Citizens in Service

Volunteers in Social Welfare
During the Depression, 1929–1941

● ● ●

• • •

CITIZENS

IN

SERVICE

Volunteers in Social Welfare

During the Depression, 1929-1941

• • •

JOHN FINBAR JONES
and
JOHN MIDDLEMIST HERRICK

MICHIGAN STATE UNIVERSITY PRESS

Copyright © 1976
MICHIGAN STATE UNIVERSITY PRESS
Library of Congress Card Catalog Number: 75–32876
ISBN: 0–87013–196–6
Manufactured in the United States of America

★
  ★
 ★
  ★
  ★

To our wives,
LOIS and KATHLEEN

Acknowledgments

Our special thanks must go to the librarians and archivists of the University of Minnesota Social Welfare History Archives, the Library of Congress, the National Archives, Butler Library of Columbia University, the New York Public Library and Schlesinger Library of Radcliffe College. Social welfare agencies, too, assisted us in our research. The YMCA, the YWCA, the Child Welfare League, Family Service Association, and the United Community Funds and Councils were among the agencies whose New York offices we visited in search of material. Individual scholars to whom we owe a debt of gratitude include Clarke A. Chambers, Gisela Konopka, Gordon Aldridge and, our favorite archivist, Andrea Hinding. We are indebted to the Rockefeller Foundation and the Michigan State University All-University Research Fund for financing part of our research. Mary Gray, Julie Hess and Judy Waligorski cheerfully typed the final draft of the manuscript. To them and many others who gave us encouragement we extend our thanks.

Contents

Tables

Introduction

In a society that believes, by and large, that every man should pay his way and, conversely, that the laborer is worthy of his recompense, the volunteer who stands in the marketplace ready for work but unwilling to be hired would be an anomaly were it not for a consistent tradition of altruism stretching back to the beginning of urban, industrial America and beyond it to greener colonial days. The tradition has been a variable one, forever adapting itself to alterations in the social, political, and religious climate, so that those engaged in good work have differed from one age to the next in the way they have gone about it. Over the past half century the face of voluntarism has again changed, partly because of increased professionalization and, more recently, the growth of subprofessions in welfare services.[1] Where this will leave volunteer participation in social service is by no means clear. In a society that is both specialized and competitive, the volunteer, if he is untrained, may be superfluous; if skilled, he may well pose a threat to others who must earn their bread. The division of labor according to expertise, which Max Weber was one of the first to note in the nineteenth century, is now a banality. The evolutionary course of specialization has tended toward the creation of a closed shop. This is as true of medicine as of carpentry, and whether the impulse toward exclusiveness lies in the need to protect the craft, the craftsman, or the consumer, the fact remains that nearly all guilds have rules governing admission. The primary social reason for regulation of practice is, of course, to protect the community from medical quacks or shyster lawyers, and modern society is unlikely to countenance a return to informal controls.

Although social work in America, in no small measure, owed its beginnings to the efforts of volunteers to provide relief for the poor and to reform society, the emergence of the paid social worker during the first quarter of this century curtailed the activity of volunteers in some ways and confined their contribution to certain well-defined areas. Social work became a profession. But the status that the social worker acquired was not guaranteed for life. The economic collapse of 1929 caused nationwide unemployment, hunger and insecurity, and in their train came the need to provide relief and more social services. Social agencies were unable to cope with requests for service and were forced to augment their staffs with volunteers.

One purpose of this study is to discover the canons of admission that applied to volunteers who entered the field of social welfare during the 1930s. How warmly volunteers were welcomed by job-conscious staff, where they served, what training and supervision they received are all questions demanding investigation.

Our ultimate purpose, however, is broader than description. Mindful of Kierkegaard's comment that the man who only recalls is a voluptuary, we abandoned our original intention of making the study a quantitative survey of volunteers in social welfare during the depression. Instead, we offer some interpretation of the historical facts concerning volunteers, 1929–1941. The fact that the study is a case history of volunteers during one decade need not act as a deterrent to broad interpretation, since in the final analysis all history is case history. Our task here is not to defend the epistemological basis of historical inquiry, but to go about the business of finding who did what, sifting the evidence, and offering our own interpretation, which must stand or fall after further investigation and other interpretations more perceptive than ours.

When describing the use of volunteers during the depression, we have deliberately avoided telling the story according to its strict time sequence. Our reasons are many. While history has its important dates, a sequential comment on these makes more sense when dealing with a longer period than ten or eleven years. Furthermore, our aim is not to write a history of the depression or even of social work at the time. Rather we wish to describe the use of volunteers in various capacities and, to do this, we have slipped to and fro in the narrative. One may object that such a method obscures development, and our only response is that history is not uniform in its progress. Besides, a strict chronology would have ruled out, or at least made more difficult, detailed consideration of diverse subjects.

A grave question facing the generation of the 1930s was the meaning of citizen participation in the context of a planned society. The debate that raged around participation versus planning was conducted in New Deal circles, at Republican gatherings, among reformers, stand-pat politicians, social scientists, and bureaucrats. In public agencies, concern for citizen participation expressed itself in the New Deal's preoccupation with citizen advisory committees and in TVA experiments in grass-root democracy. Private agencies renewed efforts to promote and justify the use of lay boards. The portion of social work most directly involved in this citizen service was community organization and administration.

The principal social welfare services that we shall consider are: (1) services of relief and care; (2) remedial services; (3) group work services; and (4) citizen services that relate to community organization and administration.

The study of social service volunteers, 1929–1941, lends itself to historical research: primary sources are available, as are secondary accounts and analyses of the era. A bibliographical essay would be out of place in this brief introduction, yet the topography of the period is such that a scrutiny of other maps is, needless to say, a necessity. The New Deal was a culmination of previous reform and, at the same time, a break with the past. The consistent interest in unemployment, labor laws, and housing that Professor Clarke Chambers has documented for the years between World War I and the depression —too long considered a vacant lot—was itself part of a tradition of concern. Historians Robert Bremner, Roy Lubove, Sidney Fine, among others, have traced the changing ideology around poverty, the abandonment of laissez-faire concepts and the growing acceptance of the need for a common welfare. Yet the crash of 1929 was unprecedented in its rapidity and vastness. Though politicians, economists, and social scientists might have looked back to the other national emergency of 1917–18 in the hope of finding a master plan that would insure recovery, the analogue was itself mischievous, as William Leuchtenburg has suggested. War and hunger, though they share the common factor of calamity, are different things. Nor did the old progressives—men such as Chase Osborn, Mark Sullivan, James R. Garfield, who had fought for reform long and hard in earlier years—bridge the old liberalism and the new. Otis L. Graham, Jr., in his brilliant study of the reformers of the progressive era who lived to see the New Deal, has dispelled once and for all any impression that the programs of the 1930s were simply logical extensions of progressivism. The historians of continuity no less than the chroniclers of change, all of them—Arthur Schlesinger, Sr. and Jr., Frank Freidel, Richard Kirkendall and Clarke Chambers—have borne testimony to the newness of the New Deal.

The specific topic of this monograph, the use of volunteers in American social welfare during the depression, has not previously been studied in detail. The selection of primary material for such a study involves a problem of affluence. There is extant in archives and agencies throughout the country a wealth of information in the form of letters, memoranda, minutes, manuscripts and drafts of articles and books, case records, research studies, conference programs and proceedings, and training manuals pertaining to the use of volunteers. Much of our research was done at the Social Welfare History Archives Center of the University of Minnesota. The Center houses major collections of significant welfare organizations and welfare leaders, including papers of the National Federation of Settlements, the National Social Welfare Assembly, the Survey Associates, the Big Brothers, Big Sisters, and the Junior League. The papers of these agencies and others in the Minnesota Archives proved invaluable for an exploration of the extent and nature of volunteer participation in social welfare during the depression. Even the gaps are interesting. The papers of the National Association of Social Workers (1918–64) contain almost no material on volunteers. The consistent concern of the predecessor groups of NASW lay with professionalization, standards, etc., and this is significant. The papers of New Deal government agencies illustrate the use of volunteers in public welfare programs. The collections—in the National Archives, of the Federal Emergency Relief Administration, the Works Progress Administration (later named the Works Projects Administration) and the National Youth Administration—contain full descriptions of federal, state, and local advisory boards. For information on volunteers in casework we searched the files of the Family Welfare Association in the New York central office of the Family Service Association of America, and the data furnished valuable clues on the use of volunteer casework aides, friendly visitors, and committees in family societies. Group work is represented in the settlement papers, as well as in the reports, studies, and manuals extant in their original form of publication or on microfilm in the New York libraries of the national YMCA and YWCA. Although our research is primarily concerned with the use of volunteers in nonsectarian agencies, we have included the YWCA and YMCA in the study, not by way of exception, but because their group work service was generally nonsectarian in character.[2] As it is clearly impractical at this point to mention all our sources, we have listed other collections of primary material, which were used, in a prologue to the notes at the back, together with the names of archives, libraries, and agencies where they are to be found.

Irving Bernstein in *The Lean Years*, an account of American labor between 1920 and 1933, broke with a tradition that dominated the writing of labor history. Instead of concentrating on the development of trade unions as institutions and their place in the labor market, he shifted his attention to the workers themselves. The result was a superb profile of the American worker in a decade of crisis. Without in any way seeking to emulate Bernstein, we draw encouragement from his methods of research, for we have sought in this monograph not to study voluntarism in general, or the evolution of voluntary, private agencies, but the volunteers who served others either directly in public and private social welfare organizations, or who contributed through service on boards and committees to the work of these agencies. Our interest is not in those few outstanding volunteers who served in the New Deal administration or who directed national agencies such as the Red Cross, but in the mass of volunteers who functioned as casework aides, motorists, club and group leaders, Red Cross chapter members, teachers in settlements, or individuals who sat on Family Welfare Association boards and case committees, National Youth Administration advisory committees, YMCA boards, and the like. We have purposely omitted volunteers engaged in fund-raising activities, although these helpers were indispensable to private agencies. The omission relates to our prime interest in volunteers who shared with professionals the common tasks of social welfare, whether in direct service or on policy-making boards. Such an approach allows consideration of the problems involved in volunteer-professional cooperation.

The center of the stage is given to volunteers in nonsectarian agencies rather than those in religious organizations. This is, of course, one of the study's limitations, for a more complete account would include the use of unpaid helpers in local church organizations as well as in national sectarian and inter-religious groups, such as the Council of Churches, the Jewish Welfare Board, Catholic Charities, and the Quaker organizations (notably the American Friends Service Committee).

There are other gaps. When writing on volunteers, we have used particular groups to illustrate our points. Such case examples are instructive; but selection is always a compromise—something is left out. For instance, much of our research on public advisory committees centered upon the National Youth Administration advisory groups, where another might have chosen to consider, say, the advisory committees that the United States Children's Bureau fostered. Again, we could with profit have given more attention to the friendly prison visitor rather than to the volunteer in the Big Brother service. This is the way of all choices, making comprehensive history, like the definitive biography, an elusive goal. But the lacunae should serve as an invitation to other social welfare historians.

Lastly, our sources imposed one severe limitation on the study: agency records, professional publications, conference proceedings, training material, and manuals bear primarily on the organization of volunteers. They tell us comparatively little about the informal, voluntary services of neighbors, friends, and relatives. We know that during the depression families borrowed from friends, relatives took care of children, grocers and landlords sometimes by necessity but often out of pity let bills and rents go uncollected, doctors attended patients free of charge, and so forth. There is a plethora of evidence attesting to this, but it is scattered in settlement records, letters and diaries, and many of the accounts are oral. We do not question the validity of such evidence—far from it—but the collection of data would have required access to a multitude of sources unavailable to us, and a different type of research.

To prevent any misunderstanding regarding the terms volunteer and social welfare, we wish to give nominal definitions of these so that the reader may know what we mean by the words. Wilensky and Lebeaux define *social welfare* as those formally organized and socially sponsored institutions, agencies, and programs that function to maintain or improve the economic conditions, health, or interpersonal competence of some parts or all of a population; they define *social work* as an occupation or profession, a group of people with more or less specific training and skills, who occupy key positions, along with other groups, in the provision of welfare services.[3] These definitions suffice for the purposes of this monograph, and we borrow them. We use the word *volunteer* simply to mean an individual, either singly or as a member of a group, who donates his time to serve others without seeking monetary recompense. In the context of this study, a volunteer must help provide some social welfare service. To rely on the differentiation of being paid or not may seem an oversimplification of the definition of a volunteer. Since it is frequently advantageous to pay a living allowance to a person offering service or to provide an honorarium for a board member, some might say that the definition of volunteer should allow for payment. However, to broaden the definition in this way would make the definition less exact. The line between a handsome living allowance and a small salary is thin. Besides, during the depression any remuneration was welcome, and people worked long hours for a few dollars. Some, again, would find the distinguishing characteristic of the volunteer in motivation, but motivation is difficult to measure. Other definitions might dwell upon negative characteristics to describe the volunteer: whereas the professional is full-time, expert, committed, the volunteer generally is part-time and unspecialized.

In summary, the study explores the extent and nature of volunteer participation in public and private nonsectarian organizations during the depression. It covers the years 1929–41. Since the use of volunteers must be seen in historical perspective, we include a chapter on volunteers from the turn of the century until the crash of 1929. The principal types of social service that we consider are: services of relief and care (Chap. 3); remedial services (Chap. 4); group work services (Chap. 5); and citizen services, which relate to community organization and administration (Chap. 6).

CHAPTER 1

• • •

The Volunteer and the Professional, 1900-1929

• • •

The Early Years

In 1903 at the National Conference on Charities and Correction, A. W. Guttridge, secretary of Associated Charities of St. Paul, suggested that the principles of evolution be applied to unpaid personnel in the field of philanthropy. He proposed a trial by nature to determine the volunteer's suitability for survival: for the time being, deny the volunteer the privilege of giving alms. "If the volunteer is not allowed to give material relief, he can do no harm with it, and he may find in this way that he has little else to give. If he has nothing else to give he is unfit to give material aid."[1] This test would not injure the poor, for they needed "not alms but friends." Should the volunteer endure, he could continue "the great undertaking of rebuilding weak character." Already, Guttridge pointed out, most of the prominent charity organizations made slight use of volunteer service for clerical work and practically none at all for scientific philanthropy's central task, investigation.

Guttridge's approach impressed his hearers. A participant from Buffalo expressed his opinion that a volunteer no less than the poor needed backbone and that too much coddling made it "as easy to pauperize a volunteer agent as to pauperize a family."[2] Mary Richmond came weakly to the defense of the volunteer with the remark that a great many professional agents began as unpaid workers. "That is one argument for having volunteers."[3]

In truth, there was at this time little interest among professional agents—and nearly all those attending the 1903 National Conference were such—in defending "honorary workers." Scientific philanthropy or, to call it by its new name, social work was, unconsciously perhaps, bent on becoming a profession, and its energies were directed to this end. The Civil War, which gave impetus to volunteer activity, also put a curb on its future development. Health and welfare agencies, such as the Sanitary Commission, a privately financed society founded in 1861 to serve the needs of Union soldiers, the United States Christian Commission, which was a YMCA organization established for similar purposes, and the Richmond Association (the Christian Commission's less powerful counterpart in the South) were all national in type and linked to complex military organizations, so that, despite the fact that the bulk of the work and its direction was in the hands of volunteers, these agencies depended upon paid staff members. This was especially true of the Sanitary Commission, whose fund-raising activities required careful planning. As a result of experiments in organization, it was logical that after the war charity should look to coordination and eventually paid assistance for its perfection.

The charity organization movement, an import from England, started out as an attempt to order chaos, to bring about the better administration of private philanthropic enterprises. The Civil War had given rise to innumerable soldiers' aid societies. New societies, pious or patriotic, had arisen since then, so that a ragtag of social services existed in most cities when the Charity Organization Societies (COS) came into being in the late 1870s. COS strove to coordinate charity and to guard its frugal treasures. To this end, it insisted upon investigation and the registration of information. Paid agents often assisted in the routine of investigation, but in the beginning they were not the mainstay of the COS movement. Lay committees determined what help should be given and assigned volunteers without special training to visit families needing counsel. Personal influence was more important to the poor than investigation, coordination, or material relief. But in time the emphasis of charity organizations began to change, as did the use of personnel. For one thing, friendly visitors were hard to find in sufficient numbers. Secondly, the reports of charity organization agents on the complexity of family problems convinced many of the movement's sponsors that the riddle of pauperism was not so easily solved and undermined their confidence in the casual reader of the *Manual for Visitors Among the Poor*. As early as 1873, at the first Conference of Charities, Mary Richmond advocated training schools for those engaged in social work, although it was not until 1898 that her dream came true with the establishment of the New York School of Philanthropy.[4]

It was almost inevitable that investigating agents, cut off by definition and actual circumstances from granting relief, should rely more and more on knowledge and technique. Almsgiving and friendly visiting by the untrained fell into some disrepute. Those who felt that all salary and no soup made poor charity did not appreciate the new manners of the Charity Organization Societies, but COS as a whole was dedicated to professionalism. Speakers at numerous social work conferences pilloried the bountiful of other generations and insisted that the indiscreet patronage of the poor give way to disciplined assistance by trained salaried workers.

The emphasis on paid expertise, so apparent in COS, did not exist in equal measure in neighborhood houses, youth agencies, or in the Red Cross, though these organizations were not wholly unaffected by professional tendencies. The Red Cross was most attached to the use of volunteers, and this outlook was due principally to its founder in America, Clara Barton. As for neighborhood houses and agencies such as the YMCA, the group work activities of these organizations and their interest in social conditions made them dependent on men and women who offered their services free of charge. A typical neighborhood house in Rochester, New York, Baden Street Settlement, recorded in its first yearly report in 1901 a list of 60 volunteer teachers for its 300 girls. They taught "plain sewing, shirt waist making, darning, crocheting, embroidery, singing and basketry," but they were also leaders of recreation and cultural groups.[5] The extent to which settlements used volunteers in the first decade of this century may be gauged by the fact that there were about 4,500 volunteer workers (exclusive of those in residence) in the 192 settlements throughout the country.[6] The YMCA from its American beginnings in 1851 glorified the role of lay leaders, not only as members of controlling boards and committees, but also as actual leaders of group activity. However, the mortality rate among associations in the latter part of the nineteenth century as well as the increasing complexity of tasks which the Ys were called upon to perform led both to centralization and to reliance on paid staff, so that Luther Gulick, a YMCA executive, could write in 1900 that an association was nothing more than its general secretary "who succeeds in extracting work more or less successfully from young men, who is the power behind the throne, nominating committees, members of boards of directors, outlining if not writing all important documents, and in many cases responsible for the financial support of the institution."[7] The birth of the word "secretarialism" in the latter part of the nineteenth century and of "secretarialization," its bastard brother, in the twentieth were signs for the alert. Between 1900 and 1920 the number of Y secretaries increased approximately 323 percent.

The volunteer, slowly learning his place, was gratefully eulogized in 1907 as "the one who stands at the surface of the water, holding the ropes and cables, and attending to the supplies, cheering by counsel and advice, while the secretary is the diver who goes down into the depths, makes the investigation and brings up the treasure."[8] But by this time there was some uneasiness on the part of paid social workers, and they were biting their lips for what had been said in haste. A special study of 150 of the largest Charity Organization Societies in the United States and Canada indicated that less than half made use of volunteer friendly visitors. It was openly acknowledged that the reaction of private charity organizations to alms giving had been excessive. Mary Richmond proclaimed that the supreme test of the trained worker was the ability to turn to good account the services of the relatively untrained volunteer.[9] The *Charity Organization Bulletin* devoted its December 1912 issue to the subject of volunteers; yet, in spite of the clear intent to laud their services, the writers showed unequal measures of trust. Moreover, the tasks suggested for volunteers tended to be ancillary to those of the professional, although they still included some home visiting and investigation.

Youth work continued to attract volunteers in greater numbers than did the family agencies. Volunteer leaders and companions were responsible for groups of individuals, but it soon became more convenient, and indeed necessary, to rely on paid staff. The staff duties varied according to the organization, its stage of development, its location, its financial position, the type of youngster it served and, lastly, the degree of staff sophistication and training. In the Big Sisters, for instance, a secretary attended the Children's Court daily and investigated cases needing attention. The secretary visited homes and turned cases over to volunteers only after making a full statement of conditions and needs. In youth work, especially of the Big

4

Sister and Big Brother type, the old principles of the charity organization movement were sometimes taken over and adapted to another setting. The 1914 annual report of the Big Sisters reads, "In these days of bureaucratic effort, often bound with red tape and rigid conventions the word 'charity' has sometimes come to have an unpleasant meaning. The great, strong factor in work of the kind done by the Big Sisters is the personal touch. In this individual interest and help is the embodiment of real charity, which often does not of necessity mean money-giving, but the giving of the heart, interest and encouragement to the child who can be helped in more than any other way by the knowledge that there is someone who cares."[10]

While being coached in the use of personal influence in the way her mother might have been in past days of friendly visiting, the Big Sister was not warned, however, about the dangers of pauperizing her young charge. In a brief summary of tangible things accomplished, the annual report of 1916 mentioned the arrangement for hundreds of children of medical and dental care, the provision of better clothing, better home conditions and proper recreation, the correction and supervision of personal habits, and encouragement in school work. The Big Sister was to use her own discretion in deciding how to help the lonely girl. The organization sought "women of leisure and opportunity, of good judgment and keen sympathies, willing to train their minds and heart for the work of rescuing and upbuilding the lives of children."

Volunteers in World War I

The outbreak of World War I involved the mobilization of a nation, and organized social work suddenly found itself thinking, talking, and using volunteers. In the face of national danger, a desire to serve and a keen sense of community responsibility motivated volunteers to join organizations aiding fellow Americans. Volunteers in the Red Cross, the settlements, the YMCA, and numerous other organizations provided soldiers and sailors with recreation facilities, canteen service, and entertainment; and when the wounded began to return, volunteer nurse's aides, helpers, and hospital visitors were at hand to comfort them. Volunteers, whether sewing, rolling bandages, providing motor transportation, or collecting funds, were indispensable in total war.

The war, with ill grace, pushed open the door of the social worker's office. Dire necessity forced secretaries of charity organizations to use volunteers in unaccustomed ways. The National Conference on Charities and Corrections urged members to introduce volunteers, not merely to friendly visiting and office work, but to casework itself. There was no reason why intelligent volunteers should not make first investigations, Mary Goodwillie of Baltimore's Federated Charities explained to the National Conference in 1915, but she added that this should be done "under the direction of a secretary."[11] Chicago's Bureau for Enrolling and Placing Volunteers exemplified the desire of social workers both to recruit and to control unpaid helpers. This bureau, which maintained contact with other social work bodies, paid close attention to policy regarding standardization of volunteer training, service, and evaluation of service.

The amount of training required of volunteers was increasing. The training of volunteers was not entirely new, but methods of imparting knowledge and skill had varied considerably in the past and had included, at one time or another, lectures, informal advice, and apprenticeship in the field. Prior to the outbreak of war, there had been little sense of urgency with regard to training volunteers. A 1913 report of the YWCA typified the leisurely approach of youth agencies. The report discussed the various factors involved in training volunteers competently enough, but it failed to make recommendations with the degree of specificity that became common a few years later.[12] In sharp contrast to the report's generalities was a paper presented at a settlement conference in 1917 that described in some detail an actual training course for club leaders at Henry Street Settlement.[13] The club leaders met once a week for three months. Their training time was divided into three periods of an hour each. The trainees spent the first hour learning crafts or domestic skills. The second hour they spent learning group games, while the third hour was devoted to lectures. These lectures covered such topics as child and adolescent psychology, vocational guidance, principles of trade unionism, and laws governing women in trades. These last two topics reflect the settlement's particular concern with labor, laws, and reform.

The conditions under which the Charity Organization Societies were willing to accept volunteers involved a rather rigorous training program. COS committee members from Chicago, Boston, and

Orange, N.J., developed a training course outline that was to serve as a model for instruction throughout the country. The outline, published early in 1916 in the *Charity Organization Bulletin,* was clearly that of a casework course with lectures, discussions, and field apprenticeship. Instruction was based largely on case records, and volunteers discussed social factors contributing to a family's problems. On the whole, the course was practical rather than theoretical in its orientation.

Once having accepted the task of training volunteers, the COS grew critical of other agencies guilty, in COS eyes, of using untrained personnel to work with families. The Red Cross, through the volunteers in its Home Service, was doing what no other welfare agency was willing or able to do—caring for numberless families in every community throughout the country. But by the very extent of its services, the Red Cross was open to the charge that it was using well-meaning but untrained volunteers to do tasks fit only for professionals. Partly to avert criticism, partly to serve families better, the Red Cross embarked on an extensive training program. Its previous safety, first aid, and nursing activities had given the Red Cross experience in both intensive and in-depth instruction, so that the information courses, chapter classes, and Home Service institutes, which it now introduced, were a natural evolution. The Red Cross relied heavily on printed material; a *Handbook of Information* was an elementary guide for beginners, and a *Manual of Home Service,* put into the hands of 100,000 readers, was a practical introduction to casework. By July 1918 no less than 25,000 volunteers had attended information classes; 6,000 volunteers had taken part in the chapter classes; and 26 institutes, held in different locations, had graduated 700 secretaries and volunteers.[14] However, the Red Cross training program was not universal; hundreds of chapters throughout the United States had not the benefit of formal instruction.

The Junior League of America was likewise concerned with the instruction of volunteers. It avoided much of the criticism leveled at the Red Cross by broadcasting its intention of training assistants and aids to professionals. Loud and clear it proclaimed its allegiance to social work goals, thus forestalling conflict.

As a result of volunteer training courses, the professional became more ready to accept unpaid help. Karl de Schweinitz of New York's Charity Organization Society in an address at the 1917 National

Conference announced the volunteer's emancipation by insisting on his right to be fired. "In employment there may be opportunity for favoritism, but in discharge all men are equal."[15] The point that De Schweinitz stressed was the necessity of judging the volunteer on his merits, with a minimum of sentiment. The careful selection, training, and guidance of the "avocational" worker made condescension superfluous and patronage an insult. The address, taken by social workers to signify the volunteer's coming of age, might have marked social work's own maturity if De Schweinitz had been fully representative of his fellows. But social work's acceptance of the volunteer was more tenuous than was made to appear at the National Conference; it was temporary and conditional on professional control.

In many respects, social work's wartime acceptance of the volunteer typified a national attitude. The war was an emergency that called for a variety of drastic changes in the nation's administration. A sense of siege, the invariable emotion accompanying all conflict, demanded that the nation mobilize—a mobilization not confined to the military, but involving the total community. In keeping with the ideology of national defense, a democratic people had to prove its commitment to democracy through corporate action. The nation had to lay aside other refinements of liberty for the time being. The War Industries Board, the War Trade Board, the Railroad Administration, the Food Administration, and the War Labor Board were all instruments to impose overhead planning, control, and cooperation in pursuance of a national goal. Once the emergency was over, the demand for citizen involvement lessened, and the social work profession, like other sectors in the community, went its separate way.

Volunteer Board Service

While the professional controlled the volunteer (for, notwithstanding De Schweinitz's egalitarian philosophy, it was the professional who could dismiss the unpaid helper), the volunteer board member was in a more secure position. The cause lay in the past. We can only understand this by turning again to the origins of social work and briefly reviewing the history of boards. Boards of directors or managers in social welfare organizations predated the Civil War. Boards were a common feature of late nineteenth century charity work, both public and private. State boards of charity, set up by governors in a number of states, typically consisted of a group of prominent citizens serving without salary.[16] These boards increased and multiplied after 1900. The boards, whose tasks originally had been mainly those of supervision, in time came to be called and to be "boards of control." In the sphere of private charity, the power of boards was greater still. COS's boards of trustees, in the 1880s and 1890s, were made up of wealthy, prestigious men, and on occasion the trustees were soundly scolded for giving charity organizations all the airs and disgraces of big business.[17] The "cautious Christian businessmen" sitting on YMCA boards at the end of the nineteenth century had minds in tune with Carnegie's paternalistic gospel of wealth. Convinced by technology and dedicated to progress, the businessmen who sat on national and local boards were unsympathetic to many of the untidy causes that professional social workers later championed. As a consequence of its links with business through its board members, the YMCA maintained a position of neutrality in labor disputes for fear of losing its wealthy patrons. The railroad strikes of the 1870s almost forced a choice on local associations, a choice between the interests of labor and management, but the YMCA leaders managed to straddle the fence. This neutrality was resented certainly by labor and possibly by the Y railroad secretaries who mixed daily with the "rougher set of men" from whose ranks they were recruited.

Progressivism was hardly a noticeable characteristic of the YMCA during the late nineteenth and early twentieth century, with the Association interpreting its social gospel in terms of service rather than reform. But whatever traces of it there were may be attributed in some measure to the Association secretaries, especially if we accept historian Richard Hofstadter's thesis that progressivism was partly rooted in the alienation of the professions and in the discontent of a ministry.[18] Conflicts arose between secretaries (drawn so often from an evangelical and badly paid clergy) and boards. The YMCA never discovered the perfect balance of power, so conflict was recurrent, and the angry comments of secretaries who during World War I accused their national board of narrowness of vision and illiberal attitudes were not without precedent.

Ironically enough, lay boards were largely responsible for the demotion of the service volunteer and the promotion of the professional social worker with his own ethics and ambitions. The notion of a tight group of paid workers struggling for status and intent on recognition is not entirely false, yet neither is it completely true. Roy

9

Lubove has suggested that social workers managed to impress upon board members the fact that wealth, social standing, and good intentions were no substitutes for training and skill.[19] The statement needs refining. Differentiation of function, by whatever name it was known (and it had a variety of titles), was a tenet of late nineteenth century business; and businessmen who sat on agency boards of trustees and advisory boards scarcely needed prompting to make charity efficient.

The Red Cross provides an interesting case history of a lay board fostering professionalization. For over thirty years volunteers in the American Red Cross, under the direction and personal care of its founder, Clara Barton, ran the organization and its operations. But accusations of mismanagement, inefficiency, and malfeasance were made against Miss Barton by her rival and successor, Mabel Boardman, in a private war waged from 1902 to 1904. The charges carried weight, not because dishonesty was proven, but because inefficiency itself was a breach of trust, and the Red Cross had failed the country by its fumblings during the Spanish-American War.

Mabel Boardman, victor, was a lady of wealth and social standing. ("I know I'm not in society because I have never seen Miss Boardman," a wistful outsider confessed.) Her connection with the Morgans, the Tafts, the Roosevelts, the Harrimans, and the Dodges—to name but a few leading families in business and government—presaged a curious alliance of capitol and capital in Red Cross affairs. Progressives were demanding high standards in government and business administration, and Miss Boardman, who believed not so much in the limitation of public and private enterprises as in efficiency and control within these institutions, modeled her quasi-government organization after big business. The Board of Incorporators and the Central Committee were of one mind with Miss Boardman on the necessity of employing paid and professional personnel. The chief of these was Ernest P. Bicknell, an experienced social worker, appointed National Director in 1908. The service volunteer waned in importance as the professional, backed by the volunteer board member, waxed strong. Time, full of little ironies, played its cruelest trick on Mabel Boardman when it later changed her from a defender of professionals into their opponent, for it meant disrupting alliances she herself had secured.

During the first World War Henry P. Davison, a banker and prominent member of J. P. Morgan and Company, accepted the leadership of the American Red Cross. The men he drew to fill the top posts of the organization were almost all volunteers and taken from large corporations, so that, as a Red Cross historian has pointed out with some pride, the roll of administrators looked like a Directory of Directors. (Among the professionals was Harry Hopkins, who, while directing volunteers, was himself subject to volunteer command. He typified what the social worker was during this period—the man in the middle.) Miss Boardman felt that professionals were attempting to take over the Red Cross and after the war joined a multitude of critics who deplored the new developments. During the 1920s she headed the Volunteer Service, a department of the Red Cross that undertook to recruit chapter volunteers for local programs and projects. The Volunteer Service bore her image. The members of her committee were women of social prominence, and the appeal of the Volunteer Service was principally to women of means and leisure. Recruitment of volunteers was slow, and Miss Boardman blamed this on professional management and the rubber stamp of a governing board, all of which reminded her of "the old days of Clara Barton."

The Decade of Normalcy

Recruitment of volunteers was slow everywhere after the war. The drop in Red Cross membership from its wartime peak of 20,832,000 to 3,012,000 in 1925 seemed to justify the opinion that the organization was "a drowsy giant to be aroused only by fire, sword, storm and flood." Gertrude Vaile, Director of Civilian Relief in the Red Cross, asked in 1918 if the various community activities that had been characteristic of the war years would survive during peacetime. One of the activities to which she was referring was Red Cross family work.[20] Her question was soon to be answered. The Red Cross Home Service that had catered to families of soldiers and sailors during the emergency—relaying information, writing letters, making provision for children without support—now began to decline, not because misery disappeared overnight, but because funds and personnel became scarce. While statistics may underestimate the number of volunteers actually engaged in Home Service work, in 1922 there were fewer than 1,000 such volunteers recorded.[21] Rural areas in particular felt the lack of volunteer family workers. Where rural volunteers were available, training was inadequate, for massive training programs were a thing of the past, leaving the rural volunteer with little more than field apprenticeship. The attitude of Miss Boardman, who became national director of Volunteer Services in 1923, undoubtedly played a part in the failure of the Home Service Corps to develop.

Of all volunteer groups in the field of social welfare none fought harder to gain independence from professional control than the Red Cross Volunteer Service under the direction of the vibrant Miss Boardman. The struggle had all the marks of a glorious revolution in which the combatants occasionally found themselves participants of a larger war between the sexes. The Junior League might have been content to train assistants for professional workers; Volunteer Service was not. Mabel Boardman did not regard social work as a profession in the way that nursing obviously was; besides, the Red Cross, in her opinion, had strayed from the straight and narrow path by becoming so involved in charitable work and by allowing itself to fall into the hands of "thousands of professionals that are now eating up its endowments and resources . . ."[22] Any woman on Red Cross salary who wished to participate in Volunteer Service had to serve in a field other than her professional one. Social work was becoming increasingly, though not predominantly, a man's profession, and men were moving into positions of administration—or, as Miss Boardman stated with greater boldness, usurping the principal offices of the Red Cross, while the women did the work.[23] "I must confess I have not such absolute confidence in the judgment of men as I might have," she wrote in a letter, adding "This is due to my past experience." Training was not common in the Volunteer Service (except in the Braille transcription program), though lip service was paid to its benefits. Indeed, since only eighteen hours of service per year were required of volunteers, there was hardly any time for training.

Statistics on Volunteer Service work are meager and depend for their calculation on the number of pins or official ensignia issued to members (in June 1926 scarcely 4,000 ensignia had been handed out), while it is likely that a considerable amount of work was done without benefit of pin. Perhaps the most valuable contribution of Volunteer Service was that it acted as a reserve corps and provided lists of available volunteers in times of emergency. But as an effort to bring the Red Cross to its senses and have it revert to a volunteer organization run by volunteers, the revolt of Volunteer Service failed. Mabel Boardman—to whom, more than any other person, the Red Cross was indebted for its organization—had built the Red Cross into a unified and effective body strong enough to resist later heresy, and the idea of wholly substituting leisured benevolence for paid expertise, however rudimentary, was heretical in the 1920s and unacceptable to orthodox boards and executives.

In the period following the war, settlement houses, too, complained that volunteers were deserting them. To gauge the exact degree of desertion is not easy; statistics, fragmentary and at times conflicting, seem indeed to indicate a decrease in the number of volunteers, but there are also tales of support and good will. Chicago's settlements, while showing a decrease in the number of its volunteers, reported that two-thirds of its resident workers, including its 317 summer residents, were volunteers giving full- or part-time service.[24] The most complete statistics on volunteer participation come from New York toward the end of the decade, 1927–28. They reveal what few other settlement statistics do—the ratio of volunteers to paid workers. During the course of one year, 74 New York settlements used the services of 1,524 volunteers, as well as 498 full-time paid workers and 950 part-time workers.[25] But the survey of 1927–28 revealed difficulties that settlement workers encountered —the irregularity of volunteers, a high turnover, and myriad problems connected with training and supervision. While doubtless there were volunteers who gave continuous service, the majority probably did not; and although some settlements held onto their volunteers for more than one season, the turnover in other houses was a hundred percent. In the settlements studied, approximately half of the volunteers were new that year. In view of these difficulties, it hardly comes as a surprise to find that ten settlements used no volunteers. The failure or inability to use volunteer services must have affected the group activities of these settlements, for neighborhood houses were generally dependent on volunteers for group leadership.

Unlike the Red Cross which in the minds of people was associated with emergency help and which therefore lost much of its support after the armistice, the YMCA entered into a period of great prosperity. Its program expanded especially in the fields of camping (this activity increased nearly fivefold from 1917–1929), organized groups and clubs, and student activities—all of which demanded maximum volunteer participation. But a struggle for control between the lay leaders and the professional staff was also taking place. Owen Pence, a Secretary of the National Council, wrote laconically, "At no time more than during the period just following the World War was the Association's claim to being a 'lay' movement more stoutly made, and more broadly denied."[26] The Y's part in the war effort had required unity in action, but the exercise in coordination had intensified authoritarian trends. A most serious indictment of Association policy and procedure was voiced in the Mark Jones Report of 1922. The report criticized the administration of the International Committee, the supreme ruling body of the Association in America. It drew attention to the decline of lay effectiveness and the prominence of the secretarial staff. "The balance of control and responsibility as between laymen and employed personnel has been completely upset."[27] The imperfections found in the International Committee reflected conditions throughout the entire organization, and the means taken to remedy these were aimed at redressing imbalance at all levels. The Constitutional Convention in 1923, seeking to implement the recommendation of the report, decreed the establishment of a National Council in which two laymen and one secretary would represent each "electoral" district. This stipulation gave the national legislative body a predominantly lay character. It did not, however, guarantee harmony in the various local and state branches, and these carried their burdens of discontent into the 1930s.

The volunteer in the YWCA was also running into difficulty. The professional staff had taken over many of the tasks formerly done by volunteers, so that little by little the effective control of many organizations belonged to professionals. Volunteers found this all the more irritating in that, by law, final responsibility for running YWCA should not have been in the hands of paid employees. Working class girls in particular lacked authority in YWCA affairs, for they had neither the time nor the skill to compete for places on the committees that made decisions concerning policy and programs. The Industrial Department undertook the responsibility of educating working girls to assume leadership roles, but did not achieve much at the time.

The service volunteer during the 1920s enjoyed prestige of sorts. He or she was the subject of reports, articles, and lectures, but was in slight demand outside the fields of recreation, group work, and fund-raising, and even in these fields was seldom without guidance from above. But it was in family and child welfare that the service volunteer was most an outsider. A 1924 report of a committee on standards for member agencies of the Child Welfare League of America stated the conditions under which (in "certain circumstances") children's agencies might employ volunteers. These were:[28]

1. The volunteer must offer definite consecutive service.
2. He must be susceptible to instruction and training.
3. The specific lines of activity must be carefully chosen and a competent executive must supervise the work.

Training, one of the stated prerequisites for service in family and child welfare, was apparently not general in the postwar period. True, social workers reminisced about the willingness of volunteers to accept instruction during the emergency, and organizations such as the Junior League made training obligatory for their members. Although some urban welfare organizations certainly promoted volunteer instruction, there is little convincing evidence that training was widespread, systematic, or thorough across the nation.

Worsening economic conditions in big cities during the late 1920s forced some agencies to re-examine their personnel policies. An incomplete study (c. 1927) of member agencies of the American Association for Organizing Family Social Work revealed that agency workers in cities with populations exceeding 500,000 were less negative in their attitudes toward volunteers than workers in smaller towns, although less than half of the societies in big cities were enthusiastic about the possibility of using volunteers.[29] This study also revealed the preferences of service volunteers in family work. The agencies were asked to list in order of popularity the types of work most volunteers preferred to do. The replies, coming from eighty agencies, may have reflected the volunteers' work experience rather than their preferences, but they do give some indication of the nature of volunteer participation in family work. These were the volunteers' preferences of activities: clerical workers (486), friendly visitors (459), transportation aides (374), casework aides (289), finance workers (195), caseworkers trained or in training (150). The friendly visitor figure is misleading: one unidentified agency alone accounted for more than a third (171) of such volunteers. Nature had dealt harshly with the friendly visitor, as A. W. Guttridge, guardian of nature's laws, had predicted.

15

Summary

Within the organized field of social service, volunteer participation declined with the advent of the professional social worker. A number of factors contributed to the dominance of the expert, not the least of which was a growing recognition of the complexity of social problems. Added to this, a repudiation of laissez-faire concepts of government by economists, sociologists, political scientists, social gospelers, and reformers in the late nineteenth century heralded the beginning of, what Sidney Fine has termed, the general-welfare state;[30] and specialized programs, which the common welfare demanded, in turn created a need for trained personnel. In private welfare, the family and child agencies were foremost in seeking professionalization, but even the settlements and youth organizations, which consistently employed volunteers, used paid staff in administrative positions. Aside from board members, volunteers assumed a less prominent role in social welfare.

The interlude of war allowed experimentation in the use of volunteer help. The nation simply could not afford the luxury of an entirely professional welfare service. Besides, the mobilization of resources was itself a commitment to democracy that the times demanded. The emergency gave an impetus to training, although the amount of education that volunteers received varied from organization to organization, and training courses were more common in cities than in rural parts. The American public had grown accustomed to specialization in the area of social problems, and it could understand the necessity of training volunteers for work in hospitals, homes, and recreation centers.

The armistice did not spell the end of concern with human want; but, unlike the handful of reformers who pressed for social betterment, the public seemed to lose interest in welfare matters, and it took a new emergency to send people back to the social agencies as volunteers—or clients.

CHAPTER 2

• • •

The New Relationship

• • •

As the 1920s came to a close in doubt, then panic, and finally depression, the status of the volunteer in social service improved. Older social workers who remembered the war again heard talk about the new relationship between the volunteer and the professional. Many felt that it was time for the volunteer to gain fuller recognition. Clare Tousley, assistant director of the New York Charity Organization Society and a hot gospeler on the subject of volunteers, spoke frequently on volunteers' behalf. The *Survey*, a journal devoted to social service and reform, was also their advocate. As early as March 1929 *Survey* editors were considering devoting a page of each issue to the topic of volunteers; however, when Clare Tousley at the 1931 National Conference of Social Work made an eloquent plea for their use in welfare work, the journal failed to publish the address. A note to the managing editor, Arthur Kellogg, reads, "AK I can't see this for us. Its philosophy is tenuous and its illustrative incidents are all in the grand New York manner, which sounds swell when Tige [Clare Tousley] tells 'em, but not so good in cold print—especially in Kalamazoo and Hutchinson."[1] But philosophy was hardly a priority when economic collapse, a farming crisis, unemployment, malnutrition, and insecurity had caused a manpower shortage in the field of social welfare. "The executive who in 1932 suffers volunteers as a necessary evil lays herself and not the volunteers open to question," wrote the persistent Miss Tousley in a later *Survey* article.[2]

Two years before the depression family caseworkers were already complaining of caseloads growing steadily heavier because of the number of people requesting relief. As unemployment mounted, the strain on agency staff became greater. From figures submitted to the Russell Sage Foundation by family agencies through the country, it appears that 51 family agencies in 48 different cities showed an aggregate of 187,000 families actively under care in March 1931, which was approximately three times the number reported by the agencies in March 1929.[3] Generally, individual agencies had three ways open to them of dealing with the situation: first, they could simplify procedures; secondly, they could delegate routine and office tasks to clerical workers or untrained aides; and thirdly, they could employ volunteers. Of 33 family relief agencies that Wendell Johnson surveyed regarding their use of volunteers during the year 1930–31, 26 reported an aggregate of volunteer workers larger than that of paid staff—1,500 volunteers compared to 1,163 paid social work staff.[4] St. Louis Provident Association, noting with surprise that employment was scarce everywhere, responded to the emergency by insisting on more rather than less home visits. This meant doubling their staff and adding 340 volunteer aides, who contributed the equivalent, in hours, of 17 workers. Through its use of volunteers the agency was able, in the winter of 1931, to carry 115 percent more cases than had been possible the previous year.[5]

Of the functions of the family agency volunteer during the emergency, Ellen Geer, president of the Association of Volunteers in Social Service, wrote, "In the family service field, which for the most part has maintained its belief in the efficacy of volunteers, service may vary all the way from the highly trained volunteer caseworker through the newly named 'casework aides' and the more generally known friendly visitors and office workers, to the humble motorist engaged in transportation work."[6]

Family agencies were not the only ones that were alive to the possibilities of voluntary service; the whole profession was discussing the topic. The manpower shortage demanded a practical solution. At the 1932 National Conference William Hodson, the executive director of the Welfare Council of New York City, protested (too much, perhaps) that social workers were realists and they would find ways of adjusting methods and procedures to the infusion of a host of untrained personnel.[7] Britain's use of volunteers was cited for the edification of American social workers. A plea by the Prince of Wales, a University of London economist told the National Conference, had had "an amazing effect": through the efforts of volunteers, university settlements and social centers were providing a modicum of work, physical training, and education for the jobless; cottage industry was beginning; people were beautifying the community; the unemployed were cultivating small garden plots donated to them; "and a very great difference will, I hope, soon begin to show in the depressed areas like the coal districts."[8] The efforts of the British were pathetically real; their hope was fervent. England, going through hard times with the rest of the world, was, like America, placing initial emphasis on everyone's native resourcefulness. Busy hands and minds would bring improvement.

Improvement remained elusive, partly because the situation was not one that a volunteer welfare army could combat effectively. In 1930 the President's Emergency Committee for Employment (PECE) sought to mobilize local effort, to promote the fund-raising activities of voluntary associations, and to coordinate the spending of private and public relief funds. Hoover appointed Colonel Arthur Woods chairman of PECE, with some thirty committee members to assist him, including Fred C. Croxton of the Ohio Department of Industrial Relations, Joseph H. Willits, a labor economist, and Porter R. Lee, director of the New York School of Social Work. Woods himself was dedicated to social service and favored many of the causes that Hoover opposed—such as Wagner's employment-service bill—but the president was determined that the committee should not invoke government intervention. And the president had his way. PECE became a citizen advisory committee in reverse, through which the government advised citizens—business, the Red Cross, the Quakers—on how to tackle the problem of unemployment and relief. Hoover opposed an appeal to Congress for any appropriation on behalf of the committee, and PECE was forced to rely on minimal funding from the Department of Commerce. Seeing unemployment as an emergency that would soon pass, PECE advocated a share-the-work policy and urged business to retain its workers on a part-time basis when jobs were scarce. The plan had some limited results in keeping men off relief, though labor rather than industry paid the piper. Woods was unsuccessful when he turned to the government for aid. Arthur Hyde, Secretary of Agriculture, turned down his request to have the department loan or distribute seed to miners with small plots of land in the drought areas of West Virginia; and the president backed Hyde. Woods was no more successful when he begged the Red Cross to assist the destitute miners of the Appalachian coal fields. Only the American Friends Service Committee was

19

willing to give PECE effective cooperation, and it was through the Quaker organization that the coal miners received what relief they did.[9]

Hoover's next committee, formed to succeed PECE the following year, was a fiasco, though the number of committee members was doubled. The choice of Walter S. Gifford, president of the American Telephone and Telegraph Company, as chairman of the President's Organization on Unemployment Relief (POUR) was particularly inept. Unlike Woods, who had a background of social service as well as business, Gifford shared with his committee members the industrialist's distrust of government intervention, and additionally had no knowledge of the extent of the nation's destitution or the nature of relief. His testimony before the Senate Subcommittee on Manufacturers in January 1932 revealed an ignorance, bordering on callousness, about the standard of relief. POUR's objectives were similar to PECE's but apart from a fund-raising campaign in the fall of 1931, the committee achieved little. Congress, unimpressed by the committee's record, refused to make an appropriation for POUR'S continuance, although the sum that Hoover requested was a pittance.

The establishment of the Reconstruction Finance Corporation (RFC) the next year was a desperate act on the part of the Hoover administration to meet a crisis as serious as war. However, while the RFC authorized loans totaling $300,000,000 to state and local governments, it stopped short of providing massive public work projects. Hoover disapproved of making RFC the vehicle of government intervention, an instrument in the hands of national planners to promote their schemes. Hoover was not alone in favoring voluntary participation over national planning. Beside the support of his lieutenants—Andrew Mellon, Secretary of the Treasury, Ogden Mills, who succeeded Mellon, and Walter S. Gifford, Chairman of POUR—Hoover enjoyed the endorsement of his own party and the cooperation of some Democrats.

Social Work in a Planned Society

How did the social work profession view the use of volunteers as a way of combatting the depression? At congressional hearings in March-April 1930, social work leaders denounced the excessive reliance on private welfare and, by implication, the overemphasis on voluntary endeavor. The hearings on the unemployment situation, in which Senators Robert Wagner and Robert LaFollett played an important part as critics of the administration, were unsuccessful in effecting the kind of massive action that social workers proposed. In other hearings less than a year later, agency officials again clamored for adequate relief and pleaded for federal assistance. Critical of the reliance on voluntary effort that Walter Gifford of the President's Organization on Unemployment Relief espoused, social work leaders demanded more radical measures. When Helen Hall testified before the committee in January 1933, she eulogized England's social insurance in the hope of having the government adopt a similar plan. Professional social workers acclaimed national planning and federal intervention through work-relief and direct assistance to the unemployed, and during the various congressional hearings a host of expert witnesses—Grace Abbott, Linton B. Swift, Jacob Billikopf, J. Prentice Murphy, William Hodson, and Harry Hopkins—voiced their approval of government participation and their discontent with purely local and voluntary endeavors to heal matters.

Roosevelt's program of social reform found its most ardent defenders among members of the social work profession. True, some social workers said that the new system of relief made it imperative that the profession concentrate on the development of professional methods and techniques, but this view did not conflict with the aims of national development. The American Association of Social Workers and the American Public Welfare Association passed resolutions on the necessity of coordinating federal, state, and county welfare, and they sought actively to enforce cooperation.[10] In 1934 AASW sponsored a Conference on Government Objectives for Social Work. The conference, held in Washington, went on record in its formal recommendations as recognizing not only social work's responsibility to promote a national program of public welfare but its duty to come up with definite methods to achieve that objective.[11]

But commitment to government intervention did not mean that organized social work abandoned the use of volunteers in welfare. In 1932 a National Committee of Volunteers in Social Work was set up as part of the National Conference itself. It aimed to draw volunteers and board members into the National Conference of Social Work and to increase the appreciation of volunteers by professional social workers.

Pressure for the use of volunteers in social service continued to mount both outside and inside the profession. Alfred E. Smith, former governor of New York and one-time presidential candidate, lent his weight to the movement by writing an enthusiastic article on volunteers in the June 1933 issue of a journal with a nostalgic title, *Better Times.* The article caught the attention of social workers. During the early 1930s the National Conference devoted a large portion of its agenda to discussion of volunteers. As the panic passed and the country settled into the depression, the tone of the discussion began to change. More thought was given to organization and procedure. In 1933 Robert Bondy of the American National Red Cross, still concerned with the question of disaster relief, suggested a methodology of rural volunteer service.[12] Hertha Kraus, speaking at the Conference a year later on the subject of German lay participation in social service, delivered what was more than a pep talk on the necessity of getting on with the job of volunteer recruitment, and asked instead whether volunteer work should not be a permanent feature of social work rather than a temporary expedient in times of a catastrophe.[13]

The entry of the federal government into social welfare in 1932 through the establishment of the Reconstruction Finance Corporation, and the expansion of the government's role in relief through the National Recovery Act a year later, brought many volunteers into public agencies. The gradual transfer of direct relief giving from private to public bodies also meant that many volunteers who previously had been attached to private agencies were now at a loose end. More than ever organization in the selection of volunteers, their training, the assignment of tasks, and supervision was needed.

Apart from the managerial problems associated with the use of volunteers, the social work profession faced other and deeper problems. Community organizers in particular, while favoring government intervention, were embarrassed by the fact that government action made community activism seem less urgent. Not all social workers shared this feeling. Mary van Kleeck of the Russell Sage Foundation, in her address delivered before the 1934 National Conference of Social Work, challenged social workers to "more decisive formulation of their purposes, more aggressive action toward their attainment, and for both of these a closer association with the workers' groups."[14] A cynic in her attitude toward political administrators who would yield only to political pressure, Miss Van Kleeck urged social workers to ally themselves with the working people and together fight economic privilege. Social workers should cease tempering their demands to the mood of Congress, and instead press for further reform.

Eduard C. Lindeman, in an address following Mary van Kleeck's, struggled with the same problem—how to guarantee citizens both security and participation. He may have intended the title of his paper, "Basic Unities in Social Work," to suggest the tenets of a common social work philosophy acceptable to the profession as a whole. If so, this was significant in view of the opinions he expressed. Lindeman, in presenting an outline of necessary social change, assumed that the American people would not lightly abandon the concept of private property or the commitment to democracy. Within this political framework, however, he recommended radical changes in the economic and social system, including a redistribution of national wealth, the nationalization of utilities, and the socialization of medicine.[15] Lindeman believed that a planned society, wedding democracy and what he called "collectivism," was possible in America.

But it was precisely in the reconciliation of diverse elements that difficulty arose. Social work theorists and administrators were in the same quandary and experienced the same stress as the New Dealers in harmonizing national planning with the citizen participation necessary in a democracy. Debate was sharpest, and tempers short, in discussion of the role of the volunteer in policy making and planning.

"The future hope in social work would be much enhanced if social workers would assume [the] basic fallacy in the idea that great welfare measures involving some 25 percent of the population can be run continuously and successfully by a bureaucratic establishment," wrote Pierce Atwater in defense of programs involving "the whole people."[16] Wilmer Shields, executive secretary of the New Orleans Council of Social Agencies, though not opposed to federal programs in themselves, took the Federal Emergency Relief Administration and the Works Progress Administration to task for negligence in the matter of lay participation.[17] Shields mentioned two prerequisites for lay participation: better understanding of the relationship between the professional executive and the nonprofessional board; and provision for lay participation to a point where its maximum usefulness might be felt.

Nongovernment agencies, too, were concerned with shared responsibility and the proper functioning of boards. The Junior League set up a committee to review the administration of the organization, and one of its charges was to draft a statement "indicating the general division of responsibility between board and executive committee, between board and staff, committees and board, and so on."[18]

Judging by the number of papers and articles published in professional journals during the late 1930s, there seems to have been an increase of interest at that time in boards and committees, perhaps because of a slackening of the emergency in which the emphasis had been on agency staffing problems. In 1937 and 1938 the *Survey* published extracts from Clarence King's do-it-yourself handbook, *Social Agency Boards and How to Serve on Them.* The author listed the chief uses of boards: interpreting agency work to the public, giving sponsorship and prestige, raising money or influencing appropriations, interpreting the community to the staff, starting new movements, giving continuity to the organization, and choosing, supervising, or removing the executive. The duties called for a sense of responsibility, and King demanded that board members be committed and informed.[19]

While the question of citizen participation exercised the social work profession, a more immediate problem for everyone in the early 1930s was the administration of relief. Not only the private organizations serving families but the public welfare agencies also sought the help of volunteers. Of 67 counties in Pennsylvania, 57 used some volunteer assistance in their public agencies. Philadelphia, with 70,000 families on relief, had a well-organized program for volunteers. The State Emergency Relief Board of Pennsylvania issued a handbook on volunteers for the benefit of its staff. The Board urged volunteers to attach themselves to agencies already in the field rather than to form new groups. In general, it was the policy of most state administrations to have volunteers work within existing structures, or, where none existed, to create a framework for coordinated effort.

Coordinated effort was not always easy. Natural barriers, such as expertise itself, separated the professional from the volunteer. Certainly by definition volunteers might be skilled or unskilled, but in fact the mass of people offering their services were without previous experience in social work. Clearly a hierarchy of skill existed, and skill—so the professional argument ran—was vital in the work of rehabilitation. Casework, especially in the family agency, was professional by 1929, and social workers took pride in the expertise they had so laboriously acquired. The predictable suggestion that there should be a division of labor, allowing the professional to take charge of families requiring intensive treatment while the volunteer undertook routine tasks of relief was not wholly realistic. The major demand was not for casework services but for material assistance. The paid staffs of family agencies were unwilling to spend their time interviewing a few clients when many more went hungry. The frustration engendered by heavy caseloads, inadequate relief, job insecurity, and the influx of large numbers of untrained workers who, it must have seemed, were just as capable as any professional of handing out food and clothes gave rise to friction in private family agencies. The heavy burden of relief that fell on the shoulders of these agencies (41 percent of unemployment relief came from private sources in 1931) soon exhausted their funds.[20] The entrance of the federal government into relief, though it meant the siphoning off of paid staff and volunteers by public welfare departments, redeemed the private agencies, and they were able to adopt a policy whereby professionals provided professional service and volunteers performed ancillary tasks. The public agencies used volunteers for the distribution of relief where regular staffs were unable to handle the task by themselves. They made use of voluntary groups to insure both the permanent stability of public welfare programs and the programs of relief work.

Unlike the public agencies, the bulk of whose workers were paid, organizations such as the YMCA, the YWCA, the settlement houses, and the Scouts depended principally upon the service of volunteers. Such agencies, once popularly known as character-building agencies, were more commonly called group work agencies during the 1930s, though that term was not acceptable to everyone. By 1929 the Girl Scouts, for instance, had already more than 26,000 volunteer group leaders under the supervision of some 300 paid workers; the Camp Fire Girls had nearly 11,000 volunteer leaders, while the Boy Scouts of America had 227,500 volunteer leaders.[21] Almost a decade later, Roy Sorenson reported to the National Conference of Social Work that, for the most part, group leaders in agencies were volunteers. In Pittsburgh 175 professionals supervised 6,330 nonprofessional workers, 91 percent of whom were volunteers.[22] When the American Association for the Study of Group Work was organized in 1936, its membership included volunteers as well as employed workers, and there were no restrictions on eligibility.

Group work agencies were especially active in the fields of recreation and education; and leisure time expanded as the depression turned workers out of their factories. The Educational-Recreation Council grew out of a meeting in April 1932 of a number of national bodies that had met at the request of the President's Organization on Unemployment Relief to prepare a recreation program for the unemployed. In September 1933 the Council formed a committee to advance cooperation in the provision of recreational services to localities. The Works Progress Administration, too, promoted leisure-time activities through its Division of Recreation, which worked closely with private organizations.

In group work agencies the massive employment of volunteers caused uneasiness. "We have so long been dependent upon untrained volunteer leaders that we find it hard to convince our supporters that adequately trained, and therefore adequately paid, leadership is essential," Arthur Swift, Jr., of Union Theological Seminary told the National Conference in 1935.[23] Swift did not propose the dismissal of untrained volunteers, but he did recommend that highly skilled group workers should train and supervise volunteers rather than devote themselves exclusively to administrative duties.[24] It should be remembered that group work during the 1930s was striving for professional recognition, so that a certain tension was inevitable in the very agencies that relied most on volunteers.

Summary

The partnership of the volunteer and the professional in social service during the depression may not have been an equal one; it was genuine nonetheless. The doubts of the caseworker, the touchiness of social work's Johnny-come-lately, the professional group worker, might be attributed with some plausibility to the reluctance of an elite to share authority, but such an interpretation skirts the many issues confronting social work during the emergency. Belief in voluntary effort allowed shades of opinion. To sort out the rights of the client to expert assistance, the duty of the professional to provide this, and the volunteer's claim to a place in the sun was difficult. If organized social work failed to come up with a solution reconciling all rights and duties, it could at least sigh that it had tried. By the end of the decade it would claim to have investigated thoroughly the relationship between the professional and his unpaid assistant. To the volunteer, of more practical significance than conference discussions were the experiments to widen the scope of volunteer service. The depression did in fact result in a new deal for the volunteer, though not all the cards dealt him were trumps.

CHAPTER 3

• • •

Programs of Relief and Care

• • •

The Settlements

The chief distress of the 1930s was hunger. A Chicago settlement house rearranged its offices to spare the feelings of clients. "Hungry waiting applicants no longer see the residents going to meals or smell the food, a situation last year almost unbearable for all concerned," a social worker wrote.[1] The cause of hunger was, of course, unemployment, and unemployment had created a new poor. One settlement house reported, "we find a new class of clients in our Dispensary clinics; women applying for Nursery care for their children, who weep with shame when they come to us for aid; mothers begging us to help find jobs for their husbands or older children; our Settlement children coming to their clubs and classes without fees because father is out of work; families moving into poorer quarters because of lower rents. Of the applicants accepted in our Nursery for the year ending March 31, 1930, about 70 percent were families where there was either total or partial unemployment."[2] Four million men were out of work in the spring of 1930; a year later the figure had doubled; a further economic crisis in 1932 brought the number of jobless to twelve million. Agencies that did not see themselves primarily as relief-giving organizations—settlement houses, family societies, the Red Cross—began feeding the hungry. Settlement houses were under pressure from their communities to grant material relief to clients. Settlement workers resented an inclination on the part of donors to discount the work of agencies not engaged in direct relief, for they were aware of the huge increase in numbers of those attending classes and clubs throughout the country, and they felt the public was ignoring the morale of the unemployed. Nevertheless, through lack of financial support, settlements had to reduce their staffs when salary cuts failed to produce a balanced budget, and volunteers, usually untrained, came to occupy positions previously held by paid trained workers. Volunteers flocked to settlement houses, as to other organizations, to offer their services free of charge, many cherishing a hope that agencies would eventually give them paying jobs. Dismissed social workers were reluctant to leave their posts and occasionally stayed on as volunteers. When government employment programs started, volunteers often became WPA workers, but job-conscious settlement employees may have greeted this development with mixed feelings, since WPA workers sometimes replaced regular staff members. The ebb and flow of employment left different flotsam on the beach at various times—untrained relief workers, professional social workers, volunteers.

The way in which volunteers were used in settlement relief work during the 1930s is poorly documented. The crisis allowed little leisure for writing, said one worker, for "too much time has had to be spent in merely seeing that our neighbors are provided with food, fuel, and shelter."[3] That unpaid helpers assisted in the provision of relief is clear, but the extent and nature of this work was seldom made explicit.

Child Welfare

Child welfare work, even during the depression, followed the 1924 policy directives of the Child Welfare League—agencies were to be circumspect in the use of volunteers, and were to offer adequate supervision. Only trained social workers, the League felt, should provide direct service to children. Although reaction to the emergency was a delayed one, eventually the depression affected personnel policies in child welfare agencies. In January 1931 the number of children under the care of the League's member agencies was approximately 39 percent more than in January of the previous year. Using as a basis for reckoning the ratio of increased work noted by League member agencies, the estimated total number of children under care on January 1, 1932, was approximately 40,000.[4] The distribution of the increase varied according to place and type of service. The increase was most marked in large urban areas, and particularly in the middle Atlantic states and in the Great Lakes region. Institutions entirely supported by private funds did not increase

29

their caseloads, simply because they did not have enough money to respond to additional demands. Quasi-public institutions had to take in the children whom the private agencies could not support. The quasi-public institutions were generally under private management but turned to state, county, or city for the partial or, in some cases, the complete support of children under care. The main burden of caring for hungry, abandoned children fell to the public agencies. The great demand for relief and the reduction of financial support encouraged the League to spell out minimum requirements for a child welfare program. Provided destitution in the home fell short of actual deprivation of food and clothing, the League was in favor of children remaining with their parents, and it argued that the expense involved in home relief for children was far less than the cost of its substitute, foster care. Since it was not until 1935 that categorical aid to dependent children became a legal right, foster care continued to be the sole alternative to starvation for children denied outdoor relief. The League, realizing that certain services would have to be curtailed for lack of funds, established priorities.

In institutions, the League considered the physical care of the child to be of prime importance; the next most important concern was "the social service program"; then came the medical program; and last in importance, though still essential, was the recreation program. It was in this last service to children that volunteers were most welcome.

Though institutions normally had their own recreation programs, children in foster care used community recreation facilities. The League recommended that, in view of the financial situation of institutions, children should make even greater use of community playgrounds and centers. It also suggested that when agencies had to dismiss paid recreation staffs, they should find volunteers to take their place.[5] The curtailment of recreation programs became common among child welfare agencies, and the use of volunteers in institutions increased as a consequence.

Recreation, however, was not the only service that volunteers provided. A Pittsburgh agency had ten groups—comprising 220 volunteers—making clothing for children; in New York volunteers confirmed interviews, made dental appointments, did office chores and, on occasion, acted as receptionists. Although residential institutions seldom employed many volunteers, two-thirds of the League's member organizations used volunteer help.[6] The League remained alert to the danger of inadequate service and begged its members to distinguish between "curtailments that will ease the present situation and those that will lower standards for years to come."[7]

Where volunteers acted as casework aides or as tutors to children, supervision was generally the rule. Some agencies envisaged the volunteer as a student responsible to a teacher. In St. Louis Children's Aid Society, each month the volunteer accounted for task and time in writing. While hopefully the social worker, through directing the volunteer, would come to appreciate the volunteer's good qualities, the center of attraction was presumed to be the social worker —"the volunteer is learning really to know the caseworker. The activities of the office, the telephone conversations, the occasional interviews that she overhears, the field work days that have their effect on the volunteer's own work, all give her something of a picture of the professional worker."[8]

Notwithstanding the vanity of the social worker who, being overheard during an interview or on the phone, felt certain of making a good impression, we cannot dismiss as irrelevant the endeavor of "focused interpretation." At any rate, judging by the public support given child welfare work, the effort was moderately successful. The child-caring organizations were conscious of the need for good public relations, and they were eager to use any interest in children. Social workers from children's institutions wooed clubs, societies, and churches. "We of the American Legion," proclaimed a volunteer as charmingly proud as the caseworker, "with over more than a million members of the American Legion and the American Legion Auxiliary, are a realistic illustration of the advantage and value of volunteers in child welfare work."[9]

Centennial celebrations lend themselves to vainglory (and the speaker was addressing a "Century of Progress" child welfare meeting), but the American Legion's self-acclaim was excusable. Its program included education of its membership and citizens at large on child welfare conditions and on the need for legislation and the appropriations of funds for more adequate standards and the improvement of facilities. The Legion pressed for the administration of emergency aid to children of veterans where local facilities were unavailable or inadequate. Also, out of its own pocket, it provided emergency relief for these children. The American Legion cooperated with established social welfare agencies and it demanded the improvement of those institutions which fell below a certain standard.[10]

With the assumption by the government of the major responsibility for relief, child welfare agencies were under less pressure to employ volunteers in their various programs, but they still continued the practice. In 1937 the League conducted a survey of member agencies to determine the extent of volunteer service in those agencies that had direct responsibility for children. Questionnaires went to 166 agencies, including children's divisions of public welfare departments, placement agencies, and residential institutions. Of the 130 agencies replying to the questionnaire, 80 reported that they used volunteer help while 50 said they did not. Of those using volunteers, 73 were private and 7 were public. Only 13 residential institutions reported the use of volunteers.

The range of volunteer activity was broad, and these are listed in Table 1 in the order of greatest frequency.

TABLE 1

Volunteer Activities in 80 Child Welfare Agencies, 1937

Volunteer Tasks	No. of Agencies
Casework aides	30
Clerical work	27
Transportation	26
Recreation	15
Special committees	12
Interpretation and publicity	4
Art, music, and dancing classes	4
Sewing projects	4
Tutoring	4
Clinic attendants	2
Shopping	2
Statistics	2
Research	1
Occupational therapy	1
Scout leaders	1
Kindergarten	1
Hospital visiting	1
Preparation of summaries	1

The table does not account for all volunteers in child welfare agencies or institutions, since it does not include professionals who offered their services free of charge. Thus, the survey excludes social workers who carried responsibility for a caseload (and five agencies reported such voluntary service) as well as unpaid medical personnel.

When we consider that child care organizations used volunteer casework aides with some frequency, the hesitation of the League to encourage volunteer casework responsibility is striking. It indicates that child welfare work was generally considered a professional function. A 1937 report of a special committee on volunteer service in children's work stated that many agencies that had used volunteers in "clinic work" found the arrangement unsatisfactory. The report called for further investigation of the question—whether volunteers could do casework. The members of the committee who drew up the report asked if caseloads could be divided in such a way that well-trained volunteers could handle simple situations.[11]

Perhaps the most interesting feature of the report was the description of the volunteer hierarchy within agencies. Large agencies found it convenient to have a chairman of volunteers, usually a board member, who was responsible for recruitment. The chairman also acted as a liaison person between the volunteers and the professional staff. In smaller agencies the executive director or a staff member took charge of volunteers.

The 1937 report, while stating the "volunteer should never replace a paid worker," set down the "supplementary services" that a volunteer might perform.[12] These included: (1) clerical services, (2) motor services, (3) shopping, and (4) sewing. The "special projects" assigned to volunteers were: (1) dental appointments, (2) tutoring, (3) music, dancing, and art, (4) debating groups, and (5) being personal friends to children. The "special committees" in child welfare agencies included: (1) legislative, (2) publicity, (3) library, and (4) employment.

The report elaborated agency etiquette—how the volunteer was to be introduced and to whom. Volunteers needed adequate facilities, including office space. Training received only brief attention in the report. In large metropolitan areas volunteers could attend either a general course on social work or a more specialized course on the function of a particular agency.

The Red Cross

The American Red Cross was drawn into the field of general relief almost unwillingly. True, by its charter the Red Cross was a relief agency dedicated to the mitigation of distress in periods of national crises, but first and foremost it was an organization whose aim was aid in time of war. With custom as a guiding star, the leaders of the organization at first refused to consider emergency relief for the jobless. They argued that, since economic distress was not a natural calamity, its alleviation was scarcely a Red Cross function. Furthermore, the organization lacked sufficient funds to launch a massive relief program, and it could not accept federal money without jeopardizing its status as a voluntary body supported by voluntary contributions. When the Central Committee in 1931 turned down the offer of government funds to supplement the organization's dwindling resources, a large segment of the population applauded its stand as being in keeping with the finest traditions of the Red Cross. The public's response to the organization's plea for help for the victims of the great drought in 1930 was itself a national vote of confidence. A hot sky and dry earth in the summer of 1930 killed cattle and withered crops in Arkansas, Kentucky, Texas, Oklahoma, and Louisiana. Throughout the Southwest drought took its toll. In the South, the drought victims were marginal farmers; many were sharecroppers; over one-third were Black. The Red Cross gave direct relief to more than 2,500,000 persons in 23 states, through the distribution of seed or food and clothing. The organization received over $10,000,000 in contributions from the public, as well as food and clothing amounting to $1,000,000.[13] National headquarters set policy, provided money and resources, and supervised relief. But the distribution of supplies was in the hands of local chapters and committees. Volunteers, numbering 37,000, worked hand in hand with nearly 2,000 paid workers from local chapters and national headquarters.[14]

The Red Cross, even as it administered a drought relief program, hesitated to become involved in massive relief for the unemployed. Officially, as late as 1932, a national program aimed at alleviating hardships caused by the depression was not sanctioned, but at the local level the Red Cross was moving from drought relief to plain unemployment relief. Cash benefits were quietly augmenting the provision of food, clothing, and shelter.

Red Cross national policy shifted significantly when the Central

Committee agreed to Hoover's request, toward the end of his term in office, to allow the organization to distribute surplus wheat and cotton. The Central Committee justified its acceptance of government surplus commodities on the grounds that goods were not the same as money. The cold and hungry were indifferent to casuistry and gladly accepted the flour and blankets. Over a million volunteers participated in this program of commodity distribution.

The New Deal profoundly altered the policies of the Red Cross. The Federal Emergency Relief Administration begot CWA in 1933, and started a trend in acronyms reflected in the titles of the alphabetic agencies and projects—WPA, CCC, NYA.[15] The government's commitment to the provision of relief meant that pressure on the private agencies to feed and clothe families of the unemployed lessened. But the intention of the administration was not to exclude voluntary bodies from the care of those in distress. Shortly after the establishment of FERA, Hopkins announced that federal relief funds might be used to provide food and work relief for hurricane victims, adding, "Relief work will be carried on in cooperation with the American Red Cross."[16] However, the government bypassed the Red Cross when it distributed surplus commodities in 1934 throughout those areas affected by severe drought. This pattern of government action had its effect on the Red Cross. Disaster relief, rather than general family welfare and public health activities, received dominant emphasis within the organization. The Ohio Valley flood in the spring of 1936 and the Ohio-Mississippi flood the next year proved to the nation and also the Red Cross itself that an organization specializing in instant help was still needed. Throughout the entire decade the Red Cross spent more than $500,000,000 on disaster relief in some 1,300 domestic operations. The organization carried on its program in close cooperation with government agencies. Interest in disaster relief varied among chapter volunteers. Concern was greatest where distress was a home town affair. In areas such as the Ohio and Mississippi valleys, where floods were a common occurrence, chapters formed committees to prepare for emergencies before they happened. In those parts of the country where storm and floods were less frequent, it was relatively difficult to drum up support among volunteers to aid in disaster relief.

Training in the Home Service owed its beginning to Eula B. Stokely, secretary of Volunteer Special Services for the midwestern area, who in 1933 pleaded with Mabel Boardman to devise a plan for

35

training volunteers for family casework. Miss Stokely, fearing a hungry winter, urged speed in setting up the program. Miss Boardman promptly responded to the appeal. She summoned to national headquarters J. Blaine Gwin, the author of a number of articles on social work, and asked him to prepare a series of elementary lectures on family casework. The lectures were published as a Volunteer Special Services manual in the autumn of 1933 under the title, "Introduction to Casework and Administration of Relief." Although Miss Boardman justified this study course on the grounds that trained volunteers would be useful in times of local disaster, in fact she recognized that it had a wider purpose, one which was stated boldly on the title page, "For the instruction and guidance of Volunteers and new workers who are active in Red Cross Home Service and unemployment relief."

Quite apart from its value to those engaged in family relief work, the manual bestowed a favor on readers in that, through its introduction, its case histories and other teaching material, it describes the work of Home Service volunteers of the period. According to this source, numerous chapter committee members were carrying part- or full-time relief responsibility. Volunteers served as assistants to professional workers. They also acted on their own, "except for the aid of field representatives in their necessarily infrequent visits."[17] From other sources it would appear that local chapters did not always welcome field representatives, and visitors from headquarters often had to resort to pleading, flattery, cajolery, "and about everything else" to make their voices heard. In many rural communities volunteers were particularly autonomous and took the lead in planning and carrying out relief programs. Relief giving was seen as a casework task, that is, "an individualized social service—for the individual or the individual family."[18] The function of casework in administering relief was to insure that the aid given would not only prevent "unnecessary suffering and starvation" but would assist families in retaining their dignity. The volunteer should make an investigation of the individual or family in need, interviewing the principal people concerned as well as collateral parties—relatives, employers, health agencies, etc.—but he should guard against "pumping" children and relatives for information. The ideal Home Service volunteer could help a family prepare a budget plan providing for necessary nutrition at minimum cost (an eternal dream), while allowing the family to make its own choice of food. Cash relief was infrequent. Much of the assistance, even the wage for emergency work, was in the form of grocery orders because they were "more easy to control."[19] The volunteer should make provision for clothing, rent, and fuel, and should not deny families these things simply because they owned a car or carried some form of life insurance—public prejudice notwithstanding. Need alone should determine the amount of assistance given. The crowning skill of any volunteer was sympathetic interviewing, since it allowed the helpless transient or unemployed father to vent his anger without risk of retribution. The interview was also the vehicle through which the volunteer made his investigation and formulated the plan of treatment. Case records, which in family agencies had become elaborate, could be short.

By the fall of 1935 some 50 chapters reported that they had held casework classes. If all these classes followed the recommendations of the "Introduction to Casework and Administration of Relief," then each group studied the topics and case histories of the manual, and discussed these with an instructor. The instructor gave class members definite reading assignments and requested them to present for consideration special questions or family situations taken from their own experience. How chapters actually used the manual, and to what extent, is not easy to determine. It was the main family work textbook of the Red Cross (re-edited and amended in 1938) and it was used throughout the country, but the reports on volunteer training sent to headquarters were often vague and incomplete. Apparently, the manual was most useful in rural areas where other means of instruction were practically nonexistent.

The Family Agencies

Closest to pain, the family welfare societies were among the first to recognize the need of emergency action to offset the harm that want and unemployment were doing to families. The Committee on Industrial Problems of the American Association for Organizing Family Social Work recommended in 1929 central planning, relief work, distribution of available jobs, centralized funding, and relief to families or individuals on the basis of need. The family agencies were also quick to see the efficacy of volunteers in countering the effects of a manpower shortage in the field of family social work. The economic aspects of the emergency made caseworkers wonder if they had identified social casework too narrowly with the effort to bring about personality adjustment through a "treatment relationship" and had ignored the therapy of bread. "We have been rudely awakened to the realization that casework is not a substitute for relief," a social worker told the New York State Conference of Social Work in 1931, "that the public agencies which supply three-fourths or more of all relief expenditures may properly be said to be doing a truly preventative job insofar as they are maintaining homes in which children are adequately nurtured; that income and economic security is itself a therapy, a prop to other securities."[20] Workers were learning to approach clients' difficulties more directly and to leave untouched those problems that they saw no possibility of treating. Many family agencies were separating their intake into groups that could or could not be treated on a purely economic basis. Trained workers took charge of intake, occupied supervisory positions, acted as consultants, or provided casework services where problems were mainly psychological. While family agencies deplored the lack of trained workers, they felt that intelligent, educated volunteers working under trained leaders at properly selected tasks could perform effectively, provided there was some guidance. Unfortunately, often there was neither time nor staff available for training.

But with or without training, the number of volunteers in family welfare organizations was increasing—volunteers served as visitors' aides, office workers, chauffeurs, and clinic escorts; they received clients and conducted first interviews; they secured records from other agencies and made out-of-town visits; they ran sewing classes and helped in nutrition centers.

A somewhat mystifying report of a self-study committee on volunteers in the Philadelphia Family Society suggests slow adjustment to the idea of volunteer service on the part of some professional family workers.[21] The report starts out with a passable description of the work of volunteers in the eight districts covered by the Philadelphia Family Society during the winter of 1931–32. When the reader is satisfied that he understands their work—visiting families, providing some medical, legal, and employment service, collecting clothing— he is told that all this is "exclusive of the emergency work." The first part of the report does not deny the emergency, it simply ignores it.

Staff discussions, upon which most of the report is based, reveal professional indifference toward volunteers.

The basic difficulty in using volunteers in family work, staff members believed, was the volunteers' ignorance of casework. Even the comparatively simple tasks most lay participants were able to perform did not give them a real understanding of the caseworker's job, making them useless as interpreters. Besides, volunteers were undependable and failed to appear when they were most needed; they lacked the sense of responsibility possessed by paid workers.

Then quietly, as though not really changing the topic of conversation, the report mentioned the depression. "We wonder whether our experience with volunteers in our emergency work this winter may possibly have something to contribute to our thinking of the volunteer as a person who can be of service to us."[22] Did the musing mean dissent? There is no break in the text to signify a disjunction of any sort, and yet the remaining portion of the report is wholly out of joint with what goes before. Whether this fact indicates different authorship or merely extreme ambivalence is uncertain. The emergency tasks of the volunteers were briefly cited as evidence of volunteer usefulness: volunteers served in many capacities—as casework aides, as messengers, as chauffeurs. The report lauded their enthusiasm just as it had previously noted their fickleness. It recommended a division of volunteers into two groups—those not involved in home visiting and those who come into contact with clients in their homes. The first group could help in clothing drives, in providing medical and dental services, and in running an employment service. The second group could aid caseworkers in their work with families, possibly by attending to the health and recreation needs of family members while the professional worker was "carrying the family on the level of social therapy."[23]

Social therapy, however, was not in the same demand as food. A survey of 75 family agencies showed that in 1932 relief needs were rapidly pushing aside consideration of other factors in family situations, and various agencies reported that in the majority of cases social workers distributed relief without reference to any treatment plan.[24] Intensive casework was possible only on a limited scale. The inability of workers to do anything but routine relief work and their frustration at the very inadequacy of relief were showing in impaired health and in growing tension among staff members. Some workers "questioned whether it is possible to adjust maladjusted individuals to a maladjusted world."[25] Long hours, nervous tension, anxiety about salaries and jobs did not sweeten tempers, and the infusion of large numbers of untrained people (both paid and unpaid) into family welfare work had demoralizing effects on permanent staff members. The strain may go a long way to explaining the churlish remark that appeared in *The Compass,* a professional social work journal, "These hundreds of emergency workers should be helped to realize that, except for the specific task for which they are employed, they have no place in the social work picture."[26]

Yet despite the frustrations of the time, social workers did try to find a place for the emergency workers. Though training was uncommon in family welfare organizations during the early depression, some agencies held brief institutes for untrained staff. These were generally simple affairs consisting of lectures and discussions covering such topics as the administration of relief, interviewing, and investigation. Agencies organized volunteer committees for definite tasks. In the main, agencies directed their efforts toward a division of labor that would provide for the fully trained professional and those workers with little or no training—for the caseworker and his aide. Cleveland's Jewish Social Service Bureau proposed a division of work that would select "those cases with good prognoses and in need of intensive case work" for the trained caseworker and would relegate the nonintensive cases to the aide.[27] The nonintensive cases were those involving chronic illness, old age, unemployment, and the like. A caseworker would screen clients. The "social examination" finished, a supervisor would conduct a treatment conference to determine whether the problems required the services of a trained caseworker. After the supervisor and caseworker had decided that a case could be handled on a nonintensive basis, they would hand it over to an aide working under the direct supervision of a caseworker. After the transfer of the case, however, the aide would be responsible for the case, though he would follow the recorded plans of the worker. The aide would attend to all clerical duties arising from the case, and make a summary recording of events.

The magnitude of the relief problem placed a strain on private family welfare agencies that they were incapable of bearing, in spite of an aggregate of volunteer workers almost equal to that of paid staff reported in a large number of agencies. The Family Welfare Association of America, whose member agencies were both public and private, urged the "sound development of family social work under public auspices," and this meant a greater public responsibility for relief. In fact, as early as 1929 public funds already paid three-fourths of the nation's relief bill.[28] A study of outdoor relief in 75 cities during the first quarter of 1931 does not indicate the same high proportion of public as compared to private relief, but it still shows that public funds provided 69 percent of outdoor relief, excluding made-work wages. If made-work wages are included in the calculation, the proportion of relief coming from private sources rises to 41 percent.[29] By the summer of 1931 private agencies were faltering, unable to cope with mounting relief costs. Several states set up Temporary Emergency Relief Administrations, beginning with New York's TERA established in September 1931, and these agencies took some of the pressure off private family welfare organizations. In 1932 Congress authorized the Reconstruction Finance Corporation to lend money to the states for direct relief and work relief, and, though the $300,000,000 appropriation was insufficient for this purpose, it made possible the establishment of more relief agencies under public auspices and set a new pattern in relief administration.[30] The Federal Relief Act of 1933 enabled the federal government to make grants to the states for relief and employment purposes. A ruling by Harry Hopkins that only public agencies should administer federal emergency relief funds fostered the rapid development of local public relief agencies. The gradual transfer of relief administration to public agencies caused many volunteers to leave private organizations. But volunteers were not the only ones who went over to public welfare departments. The Family Welfare Association encouraged private agencies to cooperate with the newly established departments, and private agencies lent their executives, supervisors, district secretaries, and caseworkers to public agencies. Government employment must have seemed more attractive and secure to professional social workers, for private agencies had neither the money to provide adequate relief to clients nor could they guarantee continued employment to their staffs.

The entrance of the federal government into the field of family welfare and employment, though it changed radically the organization and administration of relief, did not entirely edge out private agencies. A 1936 study of all the public and private agencies in Plainfield, New Jersey, revealed that, in that city of 35,000, private agencies were supplementing relief grants from the public agencies.[31] For many, the overlap of public and private agencies was a source of dismay. Benefactors were afraid that their money was being wasted, and social workers were unhappy with a situation in which clients, unable to live on the small allowances granted them by public agencies, were going from agency to agency begging for aid. There was a renewed fear of pauperism—that begging would encourage creation of permanent paupers. Gradually a division of labor evolved through which the basic activity of the private family agencies became that of casework divorced from relief, and the public welfare departments took care of the material needs of families in distress. The agreement to divide the work was tacit and never formally ratified, but the passing of the Social Security Act in 1935, when the federal government assumed even greater responsibility for the economic support of citizens, confirmed existing arrangements. This does not mean that public welfare departments only attended to the economic needs of families—in fact they provided casework services—but it does mean that they were now mainly responsible for feeding and clothing the poor. Private agencies continued to employ volunteers for the distribution of relief, but to a lesser extent than previously, and they turned their attention to other ways of using volunteers.

Volunteers in Public Welfare Services

In general, public agencies used volunteers in relief work for two purposes: first, to broaden the area of service where the volume of work was greater than the regular staff could handle; secondly, to develop grass-root support necessary for the permanent stability and progress of the work. The first purpose was the more immediate one, since the urgency was clear; but wise administrators kept in mind the advantage of allowing the public to see for itself the necessity of public programs. When thousands of families, suffering the effects of unemployment, applied to the Detroit Department of Public Welfare during the fall of 1931, the department appealed for a corps of volunteers to deliver food checks to homes. Under the leadership of the president of the Junior League, the Red Cross expanded its skeleton Volunteer Special Services. Men and women from churches, clubs, and societies joined the project. Armed with nine "dos" and "don'ts," 200 lay people entered the field of emergency relief. The

volunteer commandments (just one short of the decalogue) were:[32]
1. Be a good listener.
2. Be a good observer.
3. Report in writing all that you see and hear that you think would interest the worker.
4. Give no advice.
5. Make no promises.
6. Make no decisions.
7. Do not mention birth control or divorce.
8. Do not suggest where the client should cash checks.
9. Promise to take up with the worker whatever is bothering the person but do not say what the answer is.

The program was a practical one—to get food to homes—and the precepts given the volunteers stressed the fact that they were messengers only. A director was in charge of the volunteers working in each district. This director acted as a buffer for the friendly visitors and the paid workers when they were too busy to get the lists of calls and food checks ready for the volunteers. By employing a director of volunteers, the department avoided much of the friction between paid and unpaid workers that marked emergency relief services in some private agencies. Gradually the Detroit volunteers gained confidence and assumed other responsibilities—they helped with the verifications and investigations necessary to complete applications for assistance. The volunteers expanded their work even further and, besides the distribution of relief, they organized food and clothing collections.

Public agencies were usually eager to cooperate with voluntary bodies. In Buffalo churches and various associations organized 2,000 volunteers to assist the Department of Social Welfare in delivering grocery orders and visiting families. In Cleveland the Unemployment Relief Division, supported by public funds, used volunteers from the Red Cross and Junior League to distribute government clothing and wheat.

If volunteers were useful to city government agencies, they were even more a boon in rural districts where professional workers were scarce, caseloads heavy, and distances great. A rough survey of volunteers in Pennsylvania's public agencies showed that of 67 counties, 57 used volunteer help. That this help was not always to the liking of administrators is indicated by the following comment of a county relief director:[33]

Almost without exception the fundamental qualifications of these people for the services they are volunteering are very good, but their assurance that they know so well the people who are being helped and that they have so well in mind the dangers of promiscuous giving of food orders, has blinded them to the value of recorded facts, of uniform routine and efficiency. They frankly state that they "haven't the time for that sort of thing." As is natural, their chief interests are in their own homes and lives.

The Washington State Department of Social Security found itself unable to handle the increase in its caseload that the Social Security Act of 1935 effected. Professional social work was relatively new in the state and was almost unknown in rural areas. Department administrators invited community participation in state welfare programs, and they were especially successful in inaugurating friendly visiting services. The department designed its friendly visiting program to meet the needs of old people in particular, for over 20 percent of the old-age recipients in the state lived alone, with home ties almost forgotten—a pioneer remnant who had come to the Northwest during the Alaska gold rush. Volunteers called on the lonely and helpless. While carrying out their job of determining eligibility for social security, the friendly visitors discovered that old people needed more than a monthly check. They began to perform other neighborly services such as reading aloud to the blind, providing transportation, helping old people with their hobbies, bringing books from the library, and so on. Serious problems of health and housing often came to light through friendly visiting.

The second object of volunteer programs in public agencies—to secure community backing—was never forgotten by the Washington State Department of Social Security when it set volunteers to work. The department stimulated the growth of community welfare councils, and it was these councils that ran the friendly visiting program. In addition to the program for old-age assistance clients, practically every council carried on campaigns to develop jobs in private industry, and made surveys of community resources. Although these councils were definitely welfare councils, they were not so in the usual sense, for they sought to include not only welfare organizations but the whole community. Along with social agencies, their membership included Chambers of Commerce, PTA groups, service clubs, labor unions, fraternal groups, women's clubs, business organizations, as

44

well as local, county, and state officials. While the state department suggested practical relief projects and steered the councils into activities suited to community needs, its function was largely that of coordination. Public officials hoped that eventually the communities rather than the department would sponsor projects. They felt that the public welfare unit should participate in the council on the same basis as any other agency.

In Indiana the State Department of Public Welfare invited volunteers to assist in its program for crippled children. State and county officials cooperated with medical societies, public health nursing units, parent-teacher groups, women's clubs, community councils, and churches to take a census of crippled children. While gathering census data was the immediate objective, the goals of the program were wider, and included community involvement in state welfare programs.

The alphabetic agencies—WPA, FERA, NYA—also used volunteers to develop organizations that would effect the continuation and progress of relief projects. Most often these volunteers participated as members of advisory committees that were called upon to give advice on government programs but sometimes the committees took more direct action. In Michigan several NYA local committees assisted unemployed youth find work.

The amount of training that volunteer relief workers in public agencies received differed from place to place. In Detroit volunteers attended lecture courses and discussions; in Philadelphia they got on-the-job training; in the rural districts of Washington, where volunteer services involved "no precise technique and the only principle stipulated is friendly interest," the state prepared a manual for the volunteer visitors. The manual included basic information on the old-age assistance law, an explanation of the duties of visitors, as well as a statement on the purpose of the social security program.

Public agencies, after 1932, found themselves dealing with increased relief responsibility and with an influx of untrained personnel. There was a demand for short training courses for emergency workers. In large cities the local unemployment administration usually took the initiative in planning the orientation necessary for emergency unemployment workers. The state relief administration in many instances participated with the city administration in making and carrying out training plans, and took considerable responsibility for the smaller community, county, and town groups. In order to promote the training of emergency workers, the Family Welfare Association of America, whose member agencies included both public and private institutions, collected material from a variety of sources and organized it as an outline of a study course.[34] The course, intended for both volunteers and paid emergency workers, was a short one. The outline refers to correspondence and conferences with social workers in various parts of the country so that, with some caution, we can deduce general policies and practices relating to the instruction of emergency workers.

There seems to have been general agreement that unemployment relief workers should have an orientation in three definite areas:

1. The worker should have full and definite information about local and state resources available to the unemployed.
2. He should receive information on office routine and the formalities required by state and local relief administration.
3. He should have some knowledge of the skills needed for interviewing clients.

As the course was geared mainly to the training of "investigators" (this word occurred consistently throughout the outline), it was natural that it should have taken the bureaucratic procedures required for the establishment of eligibility for relief as the prime means of acquainting the emergency worker with casework notions and skills. Following the routine for establishing eligibility, the course outline covered the initial interview, home visits, collateral interviews, and the administration of relief.

If the training outline corresponded to the instruction given emergency workers throughout the country, then volunteers in public agencies got an education in casework that was client-centered. The investigator was to listen, to interpret and, above all, to understand that the person or family in distress was entitled to receive in full what the law set down. But, aside from the fact that the course contents may not have been so universally acceptable as the authors supposed, we are left with the realization that theory is one thing and practice another.

Summary

The circumstance that most affected the use of volunteers in relief work was not public or private sponsorship. Rather it was the nature of the service. A clear illustration of this is the manner in which public agencies, generally eager to employ volunteers in other areas, made scant use of them in child welfare. Nor was it simply the traditional position of casework, a professional method of social work. Family services, certainly in the hands of professionals, allowed volunteers, though with some reluctance, to share the power and the glory. Yet tradition had its influence. Family welfare had started as unpaid friendly visiting, and it was natural that it should revert, in a moment of crisis, to old patterns. The Red Cross, too, followed a well-trodden path, when it called upon its chapter members to assist in time of need, though it was never quite sure how far it should go in unemployment relief. Always, however, there existed a haze of uncertainty: how far could volunteers be trusted?

The nearest that social work came to safeguarding the rights of those on relief while still involving volunteers was in the organization of training courses. Much of the initiative for training emergency workers came from public welfare departments. The support that state relief administrations gave training programs was particularly important to county and small town groups that did not have sufficient funds to launch their own programs. There was great variety in the types of training that relief volunteers received, but seemingly the main emphasis was on the initial orientation of workers. At any rate, it was to meet the demand of short training courses that FWAA produced its outline for the orientation of emergency unemployment workers. The orientation outline was close in spirit to "Introduction to Casework and the Administration of Relief." The ten-week course that the outline described, while it covered the routine assignments of the emergency worker, went far beyond a detailed description of this or that task to a consideration of casework techniques. In view of the suspicion that professional caseworkers entertained concerning volunteers in family work, what is surprising about this course outline is the amount of casework lore that the volunteer was presumed capable of absorbing in ten easy lessons.

CHAPTER 4

• • •

Rehabilitation, Remedy, Restoration

• • •

The Art of Healing

Social work had as its final goal or dream the health of the total society, but more immediately the restoration of those members of the community who for one reason or another had failed to reap the benefits of the good life. Friendly visitors, and later caseworkers, endeavored to rehabilitate families; medical social workers sought to make the doctor's work worthwhile by modifying conditions that stood between the patient and recovery; parole officers counseled delinquents; travelers aid workers helped the homeless find a home —in a variety of settings social workers plied their trade of restoration. "Young as social work is, it has a glorious tradition," wrote a social worker of her own profession,[1] and that inheritance was in the opinion of many a tradition of healing. "Basically the social worker is the person who delights in individual service," a social worker told her confreres at a National Conference. "He loves to free people from their anxieties, fears, and limitations. If he is wise he strives, not so much to lift burdens from overburdened shoulders, as to draw out capacities to carry their own burdens."[2] As a reward for good deeds, the social worker was highly regarded. "He is at home everywhere, mingling freely in universities, churches, dance halls, at teas, receptions, cabarets, and in jails. He can walk arm in arm with a minister to a Methodist picnic or with a San Francisco policeman to view the night life."[3] The association with universities had given social work a scientific aura, a cause of some wonderment to the social worker himself. "The social worker is full of contradictions because . . . delight in individual service has met up with science, and the social worker must always be translating himself into the tongue of science. He speaks it well, without accent, but it is still a foreign language."[4]

Even the danger of this fluency overawing humble folk was dismissed by one admiring volunteer who saw in social workers the perfect blend of science and simplicity. "Social workers discuss their work with their peers, or teach it to their inferiors, but when they leave their own group they try to drop all shop talk and refresh their soul by forgetting that, during their eight-hour day and their gigantic overtime, their relations with people are scholarly and professional."[5]

Scholarly and professional—these two qualities gave to social work the power to influence, used freely and with effect, and the power to control. Like law and medicine, social work received its academic credentials from the university. In 1929 there were 29 schools of social work that conformed to the Standards of the Association of Schools of Professional Social Work, and all but a few of these were connected with universities. In addition to these schools, some ten other universities provided training for social work, while many more colleges and universities offered courses on social problems. Social science research was a function of the university and, while much of it was remote from the field of social work in organization and philosophy, its influence on social work was important.[6] Research in history and economics gave social workers familiarity with institutions and economic processes, their understanding of the individual was broadened by biological and psychological studies, while the research of sociologists on social pathology, community problems, and population provided a knowledge base for community organization and the administration of welfare services. More directly related to the organization of social services were the statistical and research undertakings of federal bodies, private research bureaus, and social agencies. Of varying quality and scope, these research projects, yielding hard data or soft inferences, bolstered social work's claim to being a scientific discipline. In addition to the wisdom gleaned from social science research, social work pointed to its grasp of methods and techniques of helping people in trouble as proof of the profession's authenticity. As a matter of fact, an understanding of technique rather than of research was identified as that transmissible knowledge which, according to the 1935 *Social Work Year Book*, was the first characteristic of professional status.[7] The other professional traits that the *Year Book* mentioned—recognition by outside groups, definition of function, and the formulation of common purposes—had been attained. The various social work associations, the American Association of Social Workers, the American Association of Psychiatric Social Workers, the American Association of Medical Social Workers, the American Association of Visiting Teachers, while they militated somewhat against the creation of a single fraternity, bore witness to specialization.

And specialization was most prized. Not all areas of practice were accorded the same homage, and this partly explained the readiness of social workers in one field to band together to protect or promote their status. Public recognition depended upon the development of expertise, so practitioners in a particular field tended to develop techniques and methods that were unique to that field. A case in point was the National Travelers Aid Association, which added to its professional stature by advancing the theory and practice of short-term contacts in social casework and by elaborating the principles of inter-city service to transients. But with the development of expertise came the substitution of the paid worker for the volunteer. In 1922 there were seven Travelers Aid Societies having no paid staffs; in 1937 no Travelers Aid Society was without a paid staff, although the number of societies had almost doubled. This is not to suggest that the increasing specialization in short-term contacts and inter-city service edged out volunteers. Actually, the number of volunteer groups doing travelers aid work exclusively, and cooperating with the Travelers Aid Society, more than doubled during the period 1922–1937.[8] It does mean, however, that Travelers Aid Societies came under professional management more and more, and this had been the story of most organized social work since 1900. The result was twofold: (1) better service to clients; and (2) the subordination of service volunteers to paid executives. In 1922 more organizations were doing travelers aid work than there were cities covered (608 agencies serving 557 cities), with several organizations serving single cities in an uncoordinated fashion. In 1937 changes in the type of organization and the coordination of effort had altered the situation, so that 1,227 agencies provided service for 1,832 cities.[9]

The traditions of social work, especially casework, limited the use of volunteers in rehabilitation. Areas of expertise had been staked out, and the professional claimed territorial rights. Since rehabilitation was normally carried on within agencies—family societies, hospitals, courts—or was at least agency-based, the prerogatives of the paid staff who ran those institutions were more easily safeguarded. A series of manpower studies by the American Association of Social

Workers in the 1920s and 1930s furnishes a rather extensive description of social work organization during that period.[10] One of the earliest projects of the Association, founded in 1921, was a vocational inquiry seeking information about its members and their jobs. In 1926 the Association decided to adopt the method of job analysis used in industry to study positions in social work, and this was carried out under the auspices of a committee on job analysis. The published studies are particularly useful, since they were not intended as manuals of instruction nor were they attempts to define standards and ideals, to determine what constituted good techniques, or to elucidate the philosophy underlying social work. They took the form of a statement of duties and responsibilities, relationships, qualifications, and conditions attached to the work, as these revealed themselves in the course of interviews with workers. The reports included no activity that was not customarily performed by at least a representative number of workers. The jobs examined were in family work, medical and psychiatric social service, in group work, in child care and protection, in vocational guidance and placement, as well as those positions connected with the prevention and treatment of delinquency. The volumes, *The Social Worker in Family, Medical and Psychiatric Social Work* and *The Social Worker in the Prevention and Treatment of Delinquency* were primarily concerned with remedial services, and they showed clearly the social worker's ascendancy over all unpaid helpers in this field.

The Protective Agencies

The Social Worker in the Prevention and Treatment of Delinquency gave an account of job positions that social workers occupied in probation and parole departments, juvenile courts, bureaus of policewomen and bureaus of crime prevention, in girls' bureaus and other agencies concerned with service to adolescents, in detention homes for juveniles, and in correction and penal institutions. Williamson, the author of the study, stressed the common aim of rehabilitation in all these settings when she pointed out that probation, parole, and protective work were alike in two major aspects: "they were concerned with juvenile misbehavior which had progressed beyond the control of the family, and they were concerned with understanding the individual's personality and environment in order to assist him to make satisfying and socially acceptable adjustments."[11] The National Probation Association was founded in 1906, and in the early part of the century volunteers provided the services necessary for the probation of offenders. However, by 1930 probation work had attained professional status in many communities. While volunteers frequently performed the duties of probation officers, by far the greatest number of volunteers served in "protective agencies," such as the Bethesda Society of Boston, the Juvenile Protective Association of Chicago, the Big Brothers and Big Sisters. The social work profession was dissatisfied with the number of counties that had no adequate provisions for probation services and objected to makeshift volunteer efforts to rehabilitate delinquents. The Child Welfare League of America, which was especially insistent upon professional personnel working in child care programs, urged that special probation services be set up for every juvenile court. C. C. Carstens, the executive director of CWLA told the National Conference of Social Work in 1929, "Many communities still appoint an estimable lady or gentleman without special equipment to be a probation officer but not without protest from those who have some appreciation of the services to be rendered."[12]

The protection agencies concerned themselves with social services to young boys and girls who presented problems of waywardness that threatened to turn into delinquency. In the case of girls, the problem was frequently unmarried motherhood. These agencies were of many kinds: some societies provided temporary boarding homes; others had institutions such as schools or shelters; others were simply clubs in which social workers assisted those in need of help. Accordingly, there was variation in the use of volunteers, though most societies considered volunteer services to be of great importance. Executives in protective agencies assumed responsibility for recruiting, selecting, and supervising volunteers, and they had to define the relationship between the volunteer and the professional and to indicate the types of work to be assigned to each. Recruitment followed no set patterns—volunteers were recruited by other volunteers or drawn into volunteer work through colleges, churches, and other organizations. Once in the agency, the volunteer mastered its traditions and programs, and studied protective work in general. Supervisors discussed case histories with volunteer groups to acquaint them with the work of the agency. Visits to the court and other institutions accomplished the same purpose. The manpower study of personnel in protective agencies showed that volunteers were often required to serve the agency rather than to assist the client directly. Their tasks included posting notices on bulletin boards, compiling lists of groups in the city whose activities might interest clients, doing research, keeping scrapbooks. Work that involved contact with delinquents was limited to conducting leisure-time activities or escorting boys and girls to meetings. Some agencies sought to avoid all contact between volunteers and clients. Protective agencies protected not only the wayward child but the volunteer as well.

Occupying a special position among the preventive agencies were the Big Brother and Big Sister organizations. These agencies employed volunteers to be the friends of particular boys and girls in trouble, and they insisted upon a one-to-one relationship. In 1930 many of the children—about 23 percent—were referred by juvenile court, and for them the service was an informal probation service; two percent received attention after being paroled from institutions; the majority, however, had never been arraigned in court. Referrals came from public schools, visiting teachers, parents, and welfare agencies. After a social worker or a volunteer had conducted a preliminary investigation, the decision to accept a child for help usually lay in the hands of a volunteer committee, although as a rule the executive secretary was present and participated in the deliberations. The executive secretary or the committee arranged the contact between the child and the volunteer. The helper learned the young person's story, visited his home, came to know his hopes and handicaps, and endeavored to guide him toward attainable goals. This guidance was under the general supervision of a professional worker, though the supervision of volunteers in the Big Brothers and Big Sisters was less intensive than in other protective agencies. Throughout the decade one "grand illusion" was attacked—that it was only necessary to find a boy or girl in trouble, introduce him or her to an upright citizen, and all would be well. Besides providing supervision, professional workers supplemented the work of volunteers and substituted for them in an emergency.

Since volunteers were the life blood of the Big Brothers and Big Sisters organizations, these associations paid special attention to the recruitment and selection of volunteers. Colleges, fraternal clubs, and church organizations were common recruitment centers. Some organizations relied exclusively on college students, feeling that education was a prerequisite for helping youngsters; others were indifferent to educational qualifications. In some instances, church or college groups organized their own Big Brother volunteers, and attended to the selection of candidates. More often the executive secretary of a Big Brother organization, a board member, a committee or some designated person interviewed the prospective volunteer. Personal characteristics were the principal criteria for selection. The problems of children in trouble required patience and understanding on the part of the volunteer, and the selection process aimed at finding candidates with these virtues. The turnover among volunteers was great, so that continual recruitment was a necessity. When candidates proved unsuitable, they were assigned duties not involving much personal contact with clients, such as providing transportation or clerical service. A fairly comprehensive study of local Big Brother and Big Sister organizations in the United States and Canada in the late 1930s showed that in these organizations training of volunteers was the rule.[13] Of the total number of groups using volunteers "for active case work" only three out of 51 agencies did not have training programs. The study report stated:[14]

> Individual conferences with the staff are used in almost every instance while group discussions are almost as prevalent. A great many agencies use a combination of three or more methods to complete the training of volunteer workers. Usually it is a combination of lectures, group discussions and individual conferences with the staff, and agencies employing four or five methods of training include printed material or correspondence or both.

The Hospital Volunteer

Medical social work was already some thirty years of age at the time of the depression. In 1905 it was introduced at Massachusetts General Hospital, Boston, by Dr. Richard C. Cabot, and shortly afterward at Bellevue Hospital in New York. While not built solely on Cabot's dictum that "at bottom medical ills are largely social," medical social work found in Cabot's writings much of its rationale for existing.[15] Cabot's insistence on the necessity of a social diagnosis of "the patient's malady and economic situation" had the same relevance in 1930 as it had had a quarter of a century earlier. Medical social service was firmly entrenched in the medical world in the

1930s, and medical social workers, numbering about 1,000, had their own association—the American Association of Hospital Social Workers which in 1934 became the American Association of Medical Social Workers. The educational qualifications of most medical social workers and especially of the psychiatric social workers gave these workers special status. The function of medical social service was intimately related to the practice of medicine. Although medical social service had arisen because of the dissatisfaction of physicians attempting to render adequate medical aid within the highly organized and complex institution that the hospital had become, medical social work in adapting itself to the institution had taken on quite a few bureaucratic characteristics. A social service department was not an independent organization but a subordinate part of the hospital. Policies and plans could not be worked out independently for this department, but only in relation to the total organization. This situation made hospital social workers keenly aware of the need for good working relations with the medical staff, a relationship that was most easily protected by adherence to rules, differentiation of function, and professional etiquette.

One of the duties that fell to the medical social worker in hospitals was the supervision of volunteers. These volunteers often performed tasks of a routine nature, either as clerks in an outpatient clinic or as nurse's aides helping physicians in recording preliminary medical history, weighing babies, taking temperatures, making notes. Since many medical social workers were trained nurses, this type of supervision presented few difficulties. When volunteers worked in psychiatric settings, psychiatric social workers recruited and supervised them. The duties of these volunteers were generally simple, e.g., obtaining information or attending to some routine business in follow-up.

The Red Cross was also involved in hospital work through its health aide program and its Gray Lady service. Founded in the 1920s, the Gray Lady service owed its expansion to the depression, which forced the Red Cross, beset by problems of relief coupled with a manpower shortage, to withdraw its professional staff from all Veterans Bureau hospitals and to substitute volunteer help. The service spread from government to civilian hospitals through the promotional activities of field representatives who toured the country and interested hospitals and chapters in the work. One of the selling points of the Gray Lady service, so far as hospitals were concerned, was the training given volunteers. The volunteers had to attend a series of lectures, pass a written examination, and complete a probation of at least twenty-seven hours of hospital work under supervision. Unlike the health aide program in hospitals, which languished because of professional indifference within the Red Cross itself, the Gray Ladies enjoyed the endorsement of professionals. The Red Cross was especially proud of its Gray Lady service in government hospitals, but professed some disappointment with the standards of supervision in civilian institutions. Normally, the volunteers had no nursing duties; the Gray Ladies taught English and handicrafts, wrote letters or talked with patients, but they seldom ventured to take temperatures. Yet they were very welcome in hospitals, and their services to the mentally ill, in particular, received high commendation.

In 1935 the AAMSW set about formulating a policy on the use of volunteers in medical social service departments. In part this endeavor was spurred by the Association of Community Chests and Councils, which was attempting to secure statements from various national organizations on their policies regarding the recruitment and use of volunteers. AAMSW formed committee after committee to investigate the situation of volunteers in medical social work and to formulate policy. Five years later a series of uncoordinated and diverse reports had accumulated, so the national executive committee felt that the time had come to appoint a committee of one to produce a grand synthesis. Another two years elapsed and in April 1942 the committee chairperson, Helen Hooker, wrote the executive secretary of AAMSW, "I have gone over all the back material . . . but I don't think the material amounts to anything . . . I, therefore, am writing to say that I am resigning with nothing accomplished. I feel chagrined . . ."[16]

The most complete account of volunteer service in hospitals comes not from any AAMSW research, but from a study of six hospitals that the Welfare Council of New York conducted around 1939.[17] Four of the hospitals used one or more volunteer placement bureaus in recruiting volunteers. Schools and colleges in the area also supplied volunteers. In some instances, students who worked in a hospital setting could obtain academic credits for their service. Most hospitals secured some volunteers from women's guilds and auxiliaries, social service committees, and other groups connected with hospitals. None of the hospitals studied had any formal training courses for their volunteers. Apparently, hospitals preferred untrained volunteers except for technical work, for, as one chairman of volunteers commented, too much training made a volunteer expect more responsible work than hospitals could provide. A chairman of volunteers interviewed prospective volunteers and had them fill out application forms, giving information about their educational background, work experience, and interest. In all the hospitals, staff members supervised volunteers. This supervision was informal, but it was supplemented by visits from the chairman of volunteers. Volunteers usually worked in the wards and clinics, though in one institution volunteers carried a large part of the hospital's clerical work. In one hospital, volunteers made beds, prepared lunches, fed incapacitated patients, and tidied rooms. The duties were normally simple ones but, unlike the work of the Gray Ladies, they approximated those of a practical nurse. Volunteers generally preferred work in wards and clinics; and those who did only clerical work frequently lost interest.

A job description manual issued by a Chicago volunteer placement bureau in the late 1930s or early 1940s probably summarized the position of most volunteer hospital aides when it described the volunteer's duties and responsibilities as follows: "Perform any of the unskilled duties involved in those sections of hospitals and institutions wherein the patients are attended. Has no authority and exercises no discretionary powers. Is supervised by a nurse (graduate) in charge of floor, division, department or unit."[18]

The Family Agencies

The importance of the manpower study of the American Association of Social Workers conducted during the 1920s in the field of family social work derived from the fact that this field probably embraced the largest single group of social workers.[19] The numerical strength of family workers in the practice area of casework, the most advanced of the social work methods, gave these professionals a whip hand in directing personnel policy within agencies. The use of personnel, then, depended largely on how family caseworkers viewed themselves. This self-image was not, however, the sole determining factor in the assignment of jobs. Mass unemployment had forced family agencies to switch from counseling to relief, and the distinction between the professional and his aide had become blurred. But the institution of government relief reinstated the family caseworker in his traditional role, in the private agency at least, and the position of the volunteer in family work was debated anew. Family workers viewed themselves not primarily as relief agents but as caseworkers dedicated to the rehabilitation of troubled families; and for them the early years of the depression were disconcerting in that, among other things, family agencies had been wrenched from their proper function. As Edward D. Lynde, the assistant general director of FWAA, wrote in 1935, "During the early years of the depression most family welfare societies became of necessity so involved in the administration of relief—food, clothing, fuel, shelter, and so forth—that their prime function of family casework was submerged."[20]

With the clear assumption that casework was the chief business of the family agency, social workers insisted upon the need for better equipped professional staffs. Indeed, for them, the chief value of volunteers lay not in the volunteers' service to clients but in their ability to aid and comfort the professional. Consider, for instance, the three main contributions of the volunteer to his organization listed in *Volunteer Values*, which FWAA published in 1934: (1) the volunteer brings to the staff "a renewed sense of the worthwhileness of the task"; (2) the volunteer has influence on the standards of social work in the community, and he may be a board member some day; (3) the volunteer acts as an interpreter of social work.[21] The contribution that a volunteer might make in direct service to clients was not mentioned.

The interpretation of social work to the community received considerable emphasis in the social work literature of this period, particularly by family caseworkers who felt that the public was confused about the role of the family agency. In the early period of the depression family agencies had been conspicuously connected with the administration of relief, so that even when the Federal Emergency Relief Administration took over most of the relief tasks of private agencies people continued to see private agencies as relief organizations. This made family societies stress the importance of lay participation in interpretation. Family societies relied upon board and committee members to interpret social work, but they also considered service volunteers to be in an advantageous position to look, judge, act. A personal knowledge of social work practice was the best apprenticeship for being an interpreter. "To interpret truly," the family agency volunteer was told, "and, through vital interpretation, to serve as a mediating influence between one's own social group and other groups in a community implies that one is disciplined to see what the trained social worker has learned to see, that one makes one's own analysis of the findings, and that one has the courage to face the cost of the action indicated by the findings."[22] The paid worker was armed with loyalty to, and faith in, his profession but the fact that his profession supported him made his testimony suspect. Not so the volunteer—he could speak on behalf of the professional without being accused of special pleading.

Just as Mabel Boardman had reproached her superiors for attempting to make Volunteer Special Services a means "to sell the Red Cross," so other volunteers objected to their being cheerleaders for professional teams. Many volunteers brought to the agency more than a rudimentary knowledge of social work; they had a sincere desire to give as generously as possible of their time and ability, as Mrs. Eleanor Pratt reminded the National Conference of Social Work in 1934.[23] Yet this eagerness was in many instances ignored, or the volunteer was assigned routine jobs, such as answering the telephone, addressing envelopes, and filing cards. Mrs. Pratt ascribed this indifference to professional pride and, more kindly, to the social worker's need to fight for higher standards in the midst of apathy and ignorance, but she asserted that these had produced an intolerance, a scorn of the layman, "a sort of pedantry," which was harming social work. It was unfortunate, she went on, that in a profession based upon human relationships there were members who, while handling expertly the underprivileged, failed completely to meet the lay citizen on a basis of understanding.

Not all social workers denied the charge that they ignored volunteers or gave them the most routine tasks to perform. In an address following Mrs. Pratt's, Virginia Howlett, a district secretary of Milwaukee's Family Welfare Association, acknowledged the social workers' guilt.[24] It was, she explained, an easy mistake to make in an age that prized the expert. The volunteer complained of the professional's show of superiority, though in fact he failed to discern the professional's insecurity that made him keep the lay person in his place. Miss Howlett, speaking as an agency executive, regretted this failure to welcome the volunteer, principally because bad public relations meant poor financial support. Without using the word "interpretation," she stressed its importance, possibly to convince her social work hearers. "We will not be financed unless someone knows what we are doing and believes in it. Even if we were financed from some magic gift, we could not give service if the layman, the community at least in part, did not believe in it. We cannot operate in a vacuum."[25]

In 1935 the Providence Family Welfare Society issued, as a manual for volunteers, a compilation of documents pertaining to family work.[26] The purpose of the material was to give the volunteers "some knowledge of the philosophy of case work, the programs of the social agencies in the community, the policies and functions of the particular organization for which they are working, and the relationship of various agencies to each other." The material, drawn from a variety of sources, included mimeographed and printed documents for the FWAA and excerpts from pamphlets and articles. The manual contained an article on the history of the family welfare movement, a statement of the intake policy of the Providence Family Welfare Society, a description of the type of relief given by the Department of Public Aid, articles on the philosophy of casework, an explanation of what trained workers and volunteers could do in a family agency, and some other items.[27] The tasks that family service volunteers could perform were of four kinds:

1. They could act as advisors, serving on the board of directors, on case committees, and in conference groups.
2. They could serve as clerical workers, filing, typing, doing statistical work and general office work.
3. They could provide motor service.
4. They could act as casework aides. Their duties would depend largely upon their ability and the interest they showed in assuming responsibility. Having gained some experience it would be possible for a volunteer "to assume complete responsibility for a few families."

Although the manual spoke of the casework aide assuming responsibility for families, a further explanation of the duties of the aide and those of trained workers limited the scope of the aide's work. The manual explained the responsibility of the professional worker in terms of his training and experience. It enumerated his skills rather than the tasks required of him. In contrast to the lengthy explanation of professional skills is the simple listing of direct and indirect services that a casework aide might perform.

The manual offered the volunteer guidelines for service in the form of 16 "dos" and "don'ts," most of which had been copied from other lists of helpful suggestions. These tips were intended to aid the volunteer "in working harmoniously with the policies of the agency." The agency, as an organization, played an important part in determining the activities of the volunteer. It was a means of social control, and the stress put on agency history, policies, and programs in orientation courses, manuals, and promotional literature underscores this fact. The secretary general of Milwaukee's Family Welfare Association defined volunteer service as "any activity in behalf of the agency and its clients which does not receive monetary compensation."[28] The agency was responsible for organizing services.

One of the casework aide services mentioned in the Providence Family Welfare Society was "visiting families and delivering allowances." While this suggests nothing more than the errands of a messenger boy, other sources indicate that volunteer friendly visiting increased during the depression. The recurrence of interest in friendly visiting related partly to the extension of volunteer relief work when volunteers progressed from delivering allowances to providing other neighborly services. The friendly visiting program in the state of Washington, which went beyond the delivery of relief, only showed how difficult it was to obey the mandate, "Be observant," without wishing to do something about what was observed. Agencies attempted to channel the ageless spirit of neighborliness and to modernize it. Social workers still advocated the careful selection of friendly visitors, but in the 1930s selection was less likely to be along class lines than had been the case in the early days of COS. Occasionally, clients themselves undertook friendly visiting with the approval of the agency. In another respect friendly visiting had altered over the years—the old emphasis on counsel had been replaced by a new emphasis on concrete service, and the fear of making paupers out of the poor by supplying relief and services that they might well have provided for themselves had all but disappeared. An analysis of volunteer service in the Rochester Family Welfare Society in 1934 revealed that a large portion of the volunteers' direct service to families consisted of friendly visiting.[29] Social workers were glad to hand over to volunteers chronic cases where there was little hope of improvement but where someone was needed to keep in touch with the client. However, the time that the social worker saved by delegating chronic cases to the volunteer was just as precious to the volunteer, and the hours that friendly visiting demanded made this assignment less attractive. Agencies felt that to make the service effective they had to require of each volunteer a minimum of two half days per week. Social workers complained that few volunteers were willing to accept the responsibility involved in friendly visiting.

Apart from direct service to clients, volunteers in family agencies rendered indirect service through various activity groups or committees. These committees had a variety of manifest functions as well as numerous latent ones, including interpretation. The activity groups were not administrative, although, depending on the type of activity, they had some influence on agency management. Sewing committees, clerical help committees, motor service committees, scholarship committees, publicity committees, and special gifts committees were rather common in family societies, but they were often incidental to the running of agencies. Other committees, such as business advisory committees established to consider business projects for clients or to recommend federal loans, homemaker service committees, and legal committees giving aid to clients, were more likely to influence agency policy. It was common to have a board member on important committees; frequently he served as the chairman. Business advisory committees, for instance, were generally headed by a board member. Since these committees had the function of advising on business cases and of making recommendations for loans, the rest of the membership was made up of businessmen, including where possible the director of a federal loan association. The secretary of a business advisory committee was usually a staff worker. Final business decisions, e.g., whether to recommend a loan, lay not with the secretary but with the committee. It was a division of authority according to expertise, and many of the quasi-professional committees worked in this fashion.

The case committee, occupying a unique though ambiguous place in the family agency, carried traces of its origins into the 1930s. Instituted originally to consider the needs of the poor applying to COS for help and to coordinate services, case committees later became convenient instruments for training volunteers and paid staff members. But the advent of the professional worker robbed the case committee of its old functions. Caseworkers became responsible for decisions concerning relief. Professional supervision in the field made instruction by peers seem superfluous. Still the case committee, venerable by tradition, continued on—to no certain purpose. Professionals and laymen questioned the value of any contribution that lay committee members might make to the diagnosis of a case, though very occasionally this attitude was challenged. Case committees became inactive in many agencies, while continuing to exist in the minds of board members and executives. During the depression the case committee was revived not for the purpose of advising the caseworker but to afford social workers and laymen an opportunity to discuss agency policy. The functions of the case committee were still not clear. For whose sake was policy being discussed? Were these committees advisory and, if so, whom did they advise? Did these committees set policy? Practically every agency had a case committee but no two agencies used their committees in the same way.

In 1941 the FWAA sent inquiries to approximately fifty member agencies to secure reports on the use of volunteers. It analyzed reports dealing with case committees and found that in general these committees had a dual purpose: they reflected community opinion and they had an interpretative function for the agency.[30] Whatever the manifest duties of the committee members were, agencies valued case committees principally as sounding boards and as a means of explaining to the community the work of the family society. They selected cases for discussion with this in mind. Cooperation rather than direction was sought from laymen, and case discussions, which at one time in the history of family services were meant for the enlightment of paid and unpaid workers, were now principally a means of teaching the layman wisdom.

In the late 1930s there was in family societies an intensification of interest in volunteers or—where enthusiasm had lagged—a renewal of concern. The threat of war made a manpower shortage seem likely, and social workers were already facing mounting caseloads. A committee on volunteers organized by the Social Case Work Council of National Agencies issued a preliminary report in May 1941, containing an analysis of the activities of social work agencies that volunteers could carry out effectively.[31] In one way, organized social work had benefited from the depression—it had learned in the crisis to use volunteers. Now, collecting its wits, it set about analyzing its experience and in systematic fashion proposing plans for better use of laymen. The report of the committee on volunteers of the Council of National Agencies was a lucid document that suggested jobs for volunteers, set rules, stated principles, and, unlike many earlier reports on volunteers, had a beginning, a middle, and an end. Apart from its precision and clarity, the report followed traditional lines, and none of the volunteer tasks recommended were new.

Job analysis, which had been used in manpower studies of professional personnel, was now employed in family agencies to determine the duties expected of the volunteer, the time required for each job, and the qualifications needed. In reality, few studies measured duties, time, and necessary qualifications in any complete fashion, but agency executives became more interested in empirical data. Some analyses were simply lists of possible jobs for volunteers in family societies. Others classified volunteer services and supplied statistics on personnel and the hours devoted to assigned tasks. The Family Welfare Association of Milwaukee collected and analyzed data on its volunteers, their activities, and the time spent on the job from October 1, 1939, through September 30, 1940. There is not enough evidence to say whether the Milwaukee association was typical of other associations, but the report of the finding does suggest that Milwaukee conformed in at least two respects to what we know of other agencies in the 1930s—the association made extensive use of committees and less use of volunteers in direct casework service to clients. Table 2 summarizes volunteer service in Milwaukee's Family Welfare Association for the 1939–40 period.[32]

TABLE 2

Volunteer Activities in the Family Service
Association, Milwaukee, 1939–40

	No. of Individuals	No. of Hours
Total number of volunteers	185	3,013
Persons giving committee service	130	884
Persons giving service in addition to committee work	14	2,124
Persons giving other service without committee work	55	
Volunteer services were classified as follows:		
Friendly visiting	6	54
Teaching	21	536
Recreation	6	41
Specialized	11	221
Clerical	12	431
Automobile	7	124
Auxiliary service	7	100
Toy shop service	41	621

As in the use of volunteers, so in their recruitment there was no one way common to all family welfare societies. At a Philadelphia round-table discussion in 1936 it was suggested that most agencies hand-picked their volunteers and found this to be the most satisfactory method.[33] But not all social workers shared that opinion; some of them, while valuing informal contacts with likely candidates, found such a method of selecting volunteers too time consuming to be practical. Another objection against staff members, board members, or other active volunteers personally recruiting volunteers was the danger of cliques and social exclusiveness. Agencies professed a desire to have groups of volunteers that were as broadly representative of the community as possible. At the same time, they recruited college graduates and undergraduates not only for the direct service they could provide but because in a few years those very students would be "the lawyers, the businessmen, and the politicians to whom social workers will look for support."[34] The Junior League was one of the primary sources for obtaining volunteers. A committee of Junior League members was often willing to carry some special projects in their entirety. Recruiting in civic clubs, women's clubs, church organizations, parent-teacher groups usually brought a large, though uneven, response in offers of service. Family agencies prized business and professional men as volunteers. While few agencies concentrated all their efforts on obtaining volunteers with professional training, where such men and women served, a high standard of service prevailed. In White Plains, New York, under the auspices of local unemployment committees, local lawyers, doctors, and dentists offered free professional service.

Organizations attempting to coordinate the recruitment, placement, and training of volunteers had emerged during the 1920s. These volunteer bureaus, as they were called, were generally attached to Councils of Social Agencies. Family societies found the bureaus ideal recruiting centers, as did other agencies, and worked in close cooperation with them. The objective of central volunteer bureaus was to serve all accredited social or civic agencies that desired volunteers and were properly equipped to use them. For that reason the bureaus were not affiliated with any one organization, although as a matter of fact they received special support from the Junior League, whose purpose was broad enough to foster cooperation with other organizations. The functions of a central volunteer bureau were:[35]

1. To create through participation a better understanding of social work on the part of the public.
2. To supplement and complement the services of paid workers.
3. To coordinate and improve the quality of volunteer work by serving as a source of information on all volunteer opportunities, offering guidance to applying volunteers, and placing them in jobs for which their individual interests and abilities qualified them.
4. To stimulate and advise agencies in the better use of volunteers.
5. To promote education of volunteers and board members.

Although the impetus for a community-wide organization for volunteer service usually came from a lay group such as Junior League, the central volunteer bureaus were not, strictly speaking, organizations "of volunteers" but rather organizations "for volunteer service"; consequently, bureaus had to enlist from the start the professional workers' cooperation. Bureaus emphasized the interpretation of social work in the statement of their function. Placement bureaus were popular during the depression, as their multiplication shows: between 1933 and 1941 the number of bureaus grew from eight to forty-six, almost a sixfold increase.[36] When volunteers came directly to the New Orleans' Family Service Society, they were referred to the volunteer bureau for a placement interview before being accepted. Usually, however, family agencies insisted upon interviewing applicants even when placement bureaus had screened them. The procedure was meant to protect the autonomy of the agency and to save the volunteer, not suited to the work, from the embarrassment of a later dismissal.

Volunteer bureaus did not content themselves with interviewing volunteers who sought placement, but interviewed agency executives also to make sure that volunteers would receive supervision once they had been accepted by an organization. Bureaus were quite conscious of their responsibility in this matter. Most of them would not place a volunteer in an agency where supervision was inadequate. However, bureaus recognized that not all agency staffs were large enough to supervise their volunteers in a fitting manner. Some bureaus placed volunteers who had had experience or training for a special job in a situation where they knew supervision was not of the best, but sent their young, inexperienced volunteers to agencies where supervision was superior.[37] Family agencies, for their part, were eager to provide supervision for their volunteers.

As a rule, bureaus did not require volunteers to take any instruction courses, although most offered orientation courses that approximately 75 percent of the volunteers seeking placement attended.[38] But only eight out of eighteen volunteer bureaus studied in 1935 offered any specialized instruction beyond the general orientation course.[39] This being so, family societies had to run a variety of courses, institutes, forums, and discussion groups to educate the volunteer regarding the purpose of the agency and to train him for his assigned task. This instruction was of two kinds—orientation and special training. The first type of instruction was broad; its aim was to acquaint the neophyte with the philosophy of social work in general and with the agency's policies and programs in particular. It had the advantage of helping the volunteer and supervisor find out what kind of work was congenial to the volunteer and of use to the agency. Interpretation, of course, was one of the prime objectives of orientation, "for in the event that the volunteer does not continue, she will leave the agency with a more complete picture of what it is set up to do."[40] Discussion was favored, since, besides being an aid to learning, it gave the social worker an opportunity to answer the "traditional complaints and criticisms about social work."[41] Specialized training, on the other hand, was more specific, although in small organizations it was often quite informal. Its purpose was to impart the knowledge and skill required for a particular job. Case aides, for instance, studied family service records and casework literature.

Summary

Rehabilitation rather than relief was the principal end of casework during the 1930s. Relief, insofar as it was necessary for the restoration of a family to self-sufficiency, was an important factor in the remedial process. Yet, relief never became the center of the caseworker's attention, except at the beginning of the emergency when in family agencies the "prime function of family casework was submerged." Government programs of financial relief and work relief gave back to casework its traditional role in the treatment of social maladjustment and placed family work once again among the other casework specializations devoted to rehabilitation—medical, psychiatric, court, and probation social work. That casework was professional by 1930 is plain enough; that it remained exclusively so during the depression, when demands multiplied, requires some explanation. To solve the puzzle of professional exclusiveness, two clues are offered in two words that recur consistently in the social work literature of the day. The words are "routine" and "interpretation."

Volunteers did routine tasks, carried out routine assignments, and during their volunteer hours lived lives governed by the routine of hospitals, courts, and family agencies. The charge that social workers ignored volunteers is too general to stand, but the evidence of professional statements, job analyses, course outlines, and complaints by volunteers all support the comment of a speaker at the 1934 National Conference that, "the volunteer was entrusted with only the most rudimentary and unimportant tasks, largely matters of routine."[42] Yet, whatever the motive, it was this division of labor into simple and complex tasks, that enabled agencies to operate in a period of great stress. When volunteers themselves possessed professional, business, or technical knowledge, tasks became less routine, supervision decreased, and the ban on advice and independent decision was lifted. The business advisory committees and the legal committees dealt with cases in their own way, although even here agencies controlled the supply line of referral.

At its best, the division of labor was economical and protected clients from makeshift efforts in rehabilitation; at its worst, it stifled the initiative of volunteers and fostered in social workers that sort of pedantry of which volunteers complained when they heard professionals speak in strange tongues.

The caseworker of the 1930s had a practical though not unique understanding of the importance of community opinion. What the politician or businessman knew as propaganda or promotion, the social worker called interpretation. It was a gentle name for the same thing—passing on the message. Social workers used service volunteers, committees (especially case committees), training courses, and even placement bureaus to explain their work to the community. The profession held that remedial social work demanded, above all else, expertise. That it managed to convince the public of this resulted in no small way from its constant use of volunteers for "focused interpretation."

CHAPTER 5

• • •

The Volunteer in Group Work

• • •

The Making of Group Work

Group work, which came to have a local habitation and a name in the 1930s, started out as a transient with no fixed abode and many an alias. No one claimed a method of group activity until late in the development of social work, although the phenomenon of voluntary organization seemed characteristically American. Alexis de Tocqueville, reflecting on early nineteenth century America, referred to the principle of association in his *Democracy in America*, but he was thinking largely in political terms; the phrase is almost too grand, and certainly too French, to catch the aims and acts of immigrant burial societies, fraternities, nationality groups, settlements, Protestant associations, Catholic sodalities, Jewish centers, mutual aid societies, political parties, trade unions, and youth organizations. But perhaps not. Max Weber was possibly correct in seeing in voluntary associations the bridge between the closed hierarchy of the old world and the fragmented individualism of the new.[1] Yet there is some danger in viewing voluntary associations mainly as political or even social steppingstones. The emphasis could lead easily to finding a basic unity in early group activity when in fact there was none. Often the aim of associations was not mobility but stability—the preservation of a culture or religion; and recreation quite as much as reform made men, women, and children join groups. In short, the origins, objectives, and procedures of group activity were legion and marked by diversity, not unity.

The precursors of group work came from the fields of education and recreation. Progressive education, departing from the classical traditions of learning, paid attention to child psychology, and was open to experimentation. It found its natural allies among the advocates of adult education, particularly in the settlements. The Progressive Education Association, established in 1918, served as a clearing house of information; it also gave impetus and respectability to informal education. The association's honorary chairman, John Dewey, was at once the guide and philosopher of the movement, as well as its principal spokesman. His *Democracy and Education*, which he published in 1916, was an endeavor "to detect and state the ideas implied in a democratic society and to apply these ideas to the problems of the enterprise of education."[2] The link that he forged between democracy and education was especially valuable to settlement leaders, and Dewey's writings were a justification of settlement practice. In Dewey's philosophy the criteria for judging the worth of any form of social life were "the extent in which the interests of a group are shared by all its members, and the fullness and freedom with which it interacts with other groups."[3] The settlement club, which stood for "association in its purist form,"[4] carried out its activities within a loose federation of other clubs and neighborhood groups, and its sole bond was mutual interest. Albert J. Kennedy, a settlement pioneer and head worker of New York's University Settlement, wrote in 1933, "No effort is made to turn a club into something other than it is . . . It lives only so long as members find association rewarding and desirable."[5]

But it was Mary Parker Follett, rather than Dewey, who gave group work its mystique. Her experience in the settlement, adult education, and social reform, led to her conviction that the group was an outward sign of "the great cosmic force in the womb of humanity." Mary Follett's intense and occasionally ornate prose moved readers in a way that Dewey, for all his clarity, could not. Both were interested in shared decision making and the active pursuit of social goals (surely not the stuff of poetry), but Mary Follett managed to vivify her material. Her preoccupation with "the evolving of a group idea" captured the imagination of social workers who, alas, translated her thought into a jargon that withered mystery.[6]

In large measure, too, group work owed its origins to developments in the field of recreation, although when it turned professional it lost much of the support it had previously enjoyed among national recreation agencies. In the beginning organized leisure-time activity had been associated with labor. Workingmen formed benevolent societies not only for the convenience and necessity of insurance funds and cemetery plots, but for the fellowship they found in singing and hiking together. Camaraderie had its price tag—as organized labor had to struggle for higher wages, so too it had to fight for shorter hours and free weekends. At the turn of the century leisure time for workers was one of the objectives of reformers. The recreation movement supported legislation for public parks and playgrounds, and pressed for summer camps and swimming pools for the children of the poor. The labor unions demanded recreation facilities in industry, and with some success.

Progressive education gave recreation a new twist, making it introspective. The emphasis shifted from reform to education for democracy—in effect, to self-reform through group participation. Youth organizations in particular sought to understand child psychology and to apply its principles in their programs. Psychology and sociology seemed to dictate the creation of miniature republics in which the young could learn the practice of democracy. Sometimes social action itself became primarily a means of instruction.

Eventually, the alliance of progressive education and recreation would contribute to the development of remedial group work. In the late 1930s there was an increasing tendency to use groups in dealing with delinquents in children's institutions and with the sick in hospitals, but such activity was experimental and did not conform to the prevalent philosophy of group work. A 1936 report on the objectives of group work commented on the therapeutic and correctional aspects of group work as follows: "In the use of groups in therapy, there is opportunity to observe the role of grouping itself in affecting changes in behavior, and an opportunity to see what can be accomplished with deviant persons. These are more properly objectives in research than in group work."[7] Although social workers recognized the potential of group work for therapy, and approved of the idea, remedial group work made little headway before World War II. During the 1930s group work was concerned "with ordinary, normal individuals with ordinary, normal perplexities, problems, and difficulties of adjustment in an increasingly complex world."[8]

Progressive education, recreation, and social work were each represented in the writings of Eduard Lindeman, and the synthesis he formulated contributed to the evolution of group work theory. As a young man and assistant to the minister of the Plymouth Congregational Church in Lansing, Michigan, he had organized education, labor, and recreation groups, yet despite his apprenticeship he shied away from anything that smacked of technology in the handling of

71

groups. He concentrated on enunciating a philosophy for groups and group leaders rather than on providing a systematic way of intervening in the group process itself. His philosophy was a philosophy of values, of democratic ideals "validated in action." Here, he was close to John Dewey and Mary Follett. Leisure was a school where the young learned to cooperate and create. "It would be absurd to expect American youth . . . to be staunch supporters of democratic culture if their educational experiences had provided them with no opportunity for its practical utilization."[9] Reacting against the national recreation movements of communist and fascist regimes, he feared the regimentation of leisure, and this accounts in part for his distrust of group manipulation. At the same time his concept of democracy forbade him to see in leisure a purely individualistic enterprise.

The necessity of organized administration for recreation troubled Lindeman, but he was no Thoreau and was not bent on decrying urban civilization. Certainly man had altered his environment through science and technology and had disturbed "all the natural balances." Yet there was need for social control, and this in turn made trained personnel a necessity. If children in cities were to have play space, city officials must act. Once space was available, the city had to supply play leaders. But let the buyer beware. "The moment the community employs persons to organize the recreational life of its citizens, it places authority at a new point. Administrators, organizers, leaders of play centers may now become dominators; they may become the rulers of leisure."[10] The solution to the problem lay in bringing recreation into alignment with progressive education. Only a democratic teacher could teach the young democracy.

Therefore, as late as 1929 group work was without a definite name of its own. The first volume of the *Social Work Year Book*, published that year, did not contain an article on group work although it included articles on recreation, progressive education, settlements, youth service associations, and kindred topics. The second volume in 1933 contained three short paragraphs on the subject, and the term group work was applied "to those processes of dealing with persons in groups, as in playgrounds" as well as to "the field or agencies in which this type of work is carried on."[11] The term even then had only a precarious foothold in social science literature. The *Encyclopedia of the Social Sciences,* published the following year, was silent about group work, and Paul Kellogg, editor of the *Survey,* avoided the term in his contribution on settlements to the encyclopedia. Understandably, social workers could not use the term without risk of ambiguity since sociology, elder sister to our Cinderella, had its own meaning for "group" and "group approach."[12] Recreation agencies resisted attempts to be christened anew. When a proposal was made to the National Education-Recreation Council that it change its name to the National Group Work Council, it hotly defended its right to call itself what it pleased. Small wonder! That august body included the American Association for Adult Education, the American Association of Museums, the American Library Association, the American Museum of Arts, the Jewish Welfare Board, and the National Conference of Catholic Charities. But the Council also had among its members agencies such as the Boy Scouts, the Girl Scouts, the Camp Fire Girls, the YMCA, and the YWCA which more plausibly might have used the title of group work agencies. These organizations were still called character-building agencies, but the title was losing its luster, and the agencies were groping for a new name.

The Character-Building Agencies

Character-building agencies were what they said they were—organizations that, through their recreation programs, their clubs, their informal education formed the minds and hearts of their members, especially the young. In the vocabulary of the period, leisure-time activities and character building were practically synonymous. This category of organization, according to the 1933 *Social Work Year Book*, included boys' clubs, community centers, recreation agencies, scouting and related organizations, settlements, and youth service associations. Character building covered a multitude of virtues. As a movement it inherited some of the reformist traditions of labor and much of progressive education. The lines ran parallel, converged, separated, ran parallel, and crossed over, so that at any one time it is difficult to say whether a particular agency was drawing on its democratic principles, its social action ideals, or the new psychology. Nonetheless, organizations continued to carry the marks of their origins and to be molded by their traditions. The settlements and, to a lesser extent, the YMCA and YWCA took pride in their democratic aspirations and a reformist past. The scouting organizations, the 4-Hs, the youth service agencies stressed growth, development, socialization, and borrowed heavily from child and adolescent psychology. Both types of associations used groups extensively, often exclusively. Each was very dependent on volunteers.

"The Settlement is not a critic and reformer; it is a construction. The residential nucleus of settlement workers in a neighborhood very quickly changes the surroundings and conduct in the neighborhood," the public was told.[13] The statement was no cover-up for the settlement's real activity, social action. Despite the reform ideals of settlement leaders, which Clarke Chambers has documented,[14] settlement group participation in social action was slight during the 1930s. Organized neighborhood action was rare, and political activity rarer still. In 1933 Albert Kennedy wrote, "Except in Chicago there is less participation than in the past in local, state, and national politics."[15] Service, largely group service, was the settlement's main aim and object. The 1932–33 annual report of Baden Street Settlement in Rochester, New York, makes explicit the direction that the neighborhood houses were taking: "Actual relief problems and relief giving are not ours; they are taken care of by the public and private welfare organizations, but the Settlement through its activities and by its neighborly attitude and deeds must continue to help in maintaining morale and in radiating friendly beams of human kindness amid the dark, cold atmosphere created by unemployment and dependence on charity."[16]

Was neighborliness enough? A passage deleted from a draft of the final report contained the query: "Must we go on trying to help these people accept their privations without resentment or has the future a promise of courageous and intelligent leadership which will help our country fulfill the ideas voiced for us by former President Hoover of the Children's Charter?"[17] The poignant argument that "people have to be fed but their characters can, for the time being, be left unattended" was countered with the remark that character-building agencies still had a task "in these last dreary days" to keep men and women, boys and girls "from the hideous boredom of having nothing to do."[18] The settlements drew fire from the public, who demanded that neighborhood houses hand out bread instead of cheer, but in fact they were almost bankrupt and they gave what they could. Helen Hart, of Pittsburgh's Kingsley House, showed the new face of settlements in her address to the 1931 National Conference of Social Work. She proposed six major readjustments in settlement programs, the fourth recommendation being that "the emphasis of the whole program should be on social work skills. The perfection of group relations should be as much the objective of small classes and larger recreational groups as of the clubs themselves."[19]

Albert Kennedy noted this trend toward group work (without calling it by that name) in 1933.[20] He paid homage to the settlements' cultural endeavors, their legislative and political activities, their interest in labor and industrial problems, their athletics and camps, and their neighborhood organizations, but he singled out club activity for special mention, and remarked that this was probably the sole program common to all settlements. Some of the settlements kept accurate records of the number and kind of groups they promoted. A fairly typical sample is provided in the statistical reports of Baden Street Settlement for April 1934.[21] Under self-improvement groups were these nine types with the indicated number of groups: handicrafts (26), arts and crafts (1), dramatics (1), literary (1), dancing (3), English (7), music (4), library (2), and Scouts (2). Under social groups were: storytelling (1), game room (2), and social clubs (7).

A large part of settlement work—as much as 80 percent—was concerned with youth, especially in the field of recreation. Recreation, however, was never simply recreation, at least not in the minds of its overseers. A speaker at a settlement conference in 1932 spoke of the group club as "an association of congenial people who desire to spend some of their leisure time together in activities which are preeminently recreational, but which have in them possibilities for educational development."[22]

By far the greater number of workers in settlements were volunteers. In 1930 the National Federation of Settlements had a membership of 160 settlements, with 1,500 staff members and 7,500 "volunteer assistants."[23] This fivefold majority included not only part-time helpers, but also volunteer residents. Although no conclusive evidence is available, it is likely that the majority of settlement volunteers assisted groups—in clubs, classes, scouting, and camping—since most settlement work was in fact group activity. A 1928–29 study of 166 boys' and girls' clubs in New York settlements shows that 64 (39 percent) were under the direction of paid workers; 90 (54 percent) were led by volunteers; and in 12 instances (7 percent) information as to whether the leader was paid or unpaid was lacking.[24] The proportion of paid leaders was slightly higher in girls' clubs than in boys'. The ratio was fairly consistent in the different age groups, though the clubs of members sixteen years and over had a noticeably lower proportion of paid leaders. The largest number of volunteer leaders came from colleges, schools of social work, recreation training centers, and law schools. The study report dwelt on the fact that all volunteers were professional or employed—none came from the leisure class.

The depression saw an expansion in the number of settlement volunteers. The statistical records of Baden Street Settlement, to take one example, show a steady increase in the number of regular volunteers, which reached a peak in 1934 and declined thereafter: 47 (1928–29); 38 (1929–30); 42 (1930–31); 54 (1931–32); 59 (1932–33); 66 (1933–34); 64 (1934–35); 55 (1935–36); 55 (1936–37); 28 (1937–38); 27 (1938–39); 24 (1939–40); 22 (1940–41).[25]

As the number of volunteers increased, so did the work. The ratio does not relate to Parkinson's Law but to higher attendance in all settlements and to greater demands for service. Settlements reduced the size of their paid staffs when salary cuts failed to balance the budget, and volunteers stepped into the breach. How this affected the ratio of volunteers to paid workers in group activities is uncertain; presumably volunteers played a greater part in group work, since professionals were in demand for administrative and supervisory positions. But the entrance of FERA and WPA workers into the field complicated the situation, as did the extension of settlement work to cover adult and workers' education, service to families, and community activity; so that a completely accurate assessment of the use of volunteers in settlement group work is difficult.

The settlement, being many things, was not quite typical of most character-building agencies. Its concentration on youth was in part an accident; its original mission had been wider—to serve the total community. The settlement residents thought of themselves as "neighbors" and "social explorers," their goal being to raise "the general level of civilization, more immediately for wage-earners."[26] These ideals lived, and they explain the settlements' reform activity, their child health centers, their clinics, their adult education, their cultural endeavors in drama and music, their athletic programs and camps. If the settlements came to concentrate on youth, it was because the young were simultaneously a link with the adult community the settlements sought to influence, and the promise of a brave, new neighborhood.

The Youth Organizations

Where the settlements ended in an alignment with youth, the other character-building agencies had begun. With these organizations the youth ethos was everything. They were nostalgic, romantically so, and their search was as much for the past age of innocence as for the future. The Knights of King Arthur, the Princely Knights of Character Castle, the Order of Sir Galahad, Inc., the Sons of Daniel Boone, and Woodcraft Indians gave way to the Pathfinders of America, the Boy Scouts, Girl Scouts, and Camp Fire Girls, but the symbols were still camps and castles, codes of honor and pledges of loyalty. As the frontier closed, boys and their fathers could dispense with Arthur and the Knights of the Round Table and dream instead of Daniel Boone and the pioneers, so that the back-to-nature theme, which was part and parcel of the movement, could be expressed in a native way.

Yet romance and nostalgia was not all there was to the character-building organizations, however persistent the motif. Commenting on the rise of youth organizations in the decade between 1910 and 1920—the Boy Scouts, Girl Scouts, Camp Fire Girls, 4-H Clubs, Boy Rangers, Pioneer Youth of America—Grace Coyle noted a similarity of pattern. "They are geared to and are successful with young in the pre-adolescent and early adolescent period. They are all one-sex organizations and serve to create bonds between those of the same sex in the period just before heterosexual interests develop."[27] Miss Coyle, drawing on psychology and sociology to explain the phenomenon, believed that when economic conditions and educational requirements commonly necessitated postponement of marriage at least ten years after puberty, the programs of the youth organizations served to delay psychosexual maturation, to sublimate needs and direct them into activities sanctioned by the community as appropriate to early adolescence. The fact that these programs were most successful with middle-class youth, she concluded, indicated that the middle class had a vested interest in sublimation.

The theory is not without its merits, though the explanation was more popular in the 1940s than in the three earlier decades. The character-building agencies did stress developmental psychology and were not blind to the meaning of symbols and ritual. But, consciously at least, their efforts were devoted to development and maturation, teaching boys how to be boys and later men, and girls how to grow to be wives and mothers. The emphasis on one-sex peer relations gives some substance, however, to Grace Coyle's speculation. From a sociological point of view, Coyle's position is quite tenable. Character-building organizations formed a bridge between the child's home and the factory or office.

The youth organizations relied on volunteers as a matter of course. Volunteers, whether in boys' clubs, Scout troops, or the Ys, directed group activity. They were called group leaders, group advisors, scoutmasters, den chiefs, but seldom social group workers. That name became popular only after group work had established itself in the 1930s and the title was used sparingly. The tasks that volunteers performed varied from organization to organization, and included physical education and recreation, household arts, crafts, dramatics, teaching languages and music, as well as directing miscellaneous interest groups, clubs, and troops. There was a tendency in some agencies—the YWCA, for instance—to differentiate, on the basis of training, specialists from general service volunteers. Thus project directors engaged in pottery or woodcraft, and teachers of domestic science or music were called program volunteers in the YWCA. The association expected the specialist not only to be able to adapt herself to a group but also to be mistress of her craft. However, as group work moved away from education and recreation—and the gap widened in the late 1920s and early 1930s—the ordinary group leader, rather than the specialist, received most attention from the social work profession. And the group leader was normally a volunteer.

Margaret Williamson in a manpower study of social workers, published in 1929, analyzed the jobs of executives, directors, and specialists, but purposely left out of consideration the group leader, i.e., "the person in charge of hand-to-hand, face-to-face guidance of a particular group," since his job was "usually volunteer or part-time work."[28] Because the aim of the study was to examine only those tasks that were performed by a representative number of professionals, the exclusion was logical.

Professional group leadership did not increase appreciably during the 1930s, though there may have been some gains in particular instances. Reporting on the findings of several studies before the National Conference of Social Work, Roy Sorenson in 1937 concluded that the bulk of "direct leadership" in group work agencies was still unprofessional and largely volunteer.[29] The depression forced many agencies to reduce their paid staffs and hand over the direction of activities to volunteers. For instance, in 1936 the association secretariat of the YMCA stood at approximately 70 percent of 1929 levels; in 1929 the secretariat numbered 4,720, while in 1936 the figure was 3,480.[30] From material supplied by the National Council, L. L. McClow traced three years' decline of paid leadership and the increase in volunteer leadership in the YMCA, as shown in Table 3.[31]

TABLE 3

Ratio of Paid to Unpaid Workers in the YMCA, 1934–36

Paid Leaders	1934	1935	1936
Secretaries	12.3%	8.7%	6.9%
Others	6.3	8.5	9.5
Total	18.6	17.2	16.4
Volunteer Leaders			
Within the group	43.1	38.3	46.0
Outside the group	38.3	44.5	37.6
Total	81.4	82.8	83.6

As might be expected, the leadership of the scouting movement was predominately volunteer. In 1935–36 the Boy Scouts of America, with a membership of approximately 1,000,000 boys, had only 800 paid scout executives of various rank, while its volunteer adult leaders in charge of regular group activities numbered 250,000. The Girl Scouts, numbering approximately 400,000, were led by 50,000 adult leaders of whom less than two percent were paid professional workers.[32]

The only statistics that show a lower ratio of volunteer helpers in fields of service that the American Association of Social Workers identified with group work are those relating to boys' clubs and the "playground and recreation systems." But the figures that the American Youth Commission collected in its study of boys' clubs and the statistics of the National Recreation Association are ambiguous and do not allow a sufficient distinction between administration and direct leadership of groups. However, the statistics of the National Recreation Association, even if they do not contradict the findings of AASW's manpower study bring to mind a more fundamental objection to some of AASW's assumptions in conducting its job analysis of group work personnel. The assumption that group work was any and all leisure-time activity in a group, conducted under the eye of a group director "trained in activities and processes thought to be developmental," was a gratuitous assumption, and it led to the inclusion of the "playground and recreation systems" among the natural group work settings.[33] Williamson made group workers out of playground superintendents, directors and supervisors of recreation, and play leaders. Recreation leaders thought otherwise. The National Education-Recreation Council, in refusing to become the National Group Work Council, pledged its allegiance not to social work but to education and recreation "broadly conceived."[34] Slighted by the "mass recreation" movement, social group work went ahead with its own plans.

In Search of a Profession

When universities and colleges began to take an interest, the future professional status of group work was virtually assured. In 1923 the School of Applied Social Sciences at Western Reserve University, Cleveland, offered a "Group Service Training Course," the first of its kind. Within a short time the course, limited to graduates, had strict entrance requirements, including an undergraduate major in the social sciences. Other institutions quickly followed Western Reserve's example and organized group work courses, often in partnership with neighboring agencies in which students were required to do field work. Northwestern University, the University of Minnesota, the Carnegie Institute of Technology, George William College, and Springfield College (these last two run by the YMCA) pioneered in group work education. A decade later no fewer than thirty-three schools offered one or more courses on a graduate or professional level. Most of the institutions were schools of social work, and their catalogues assumed that the new discipline belonged to social work, although there was no universal agreement on this point.

Decked in cap and gown, the specialty became known officially as social group work or, more familiarly among intimates, as group work. Close relatives quarreled with the choice of name. The National Recreation Association in particular was upset, and canvassed its members for their opinions. Letters to Howard Braucher of NRA revealed a common dislike for the new name[35] but, as one correspondent admitted, "the flight from character building as a term" had already begun,[36] and youth organizations were openly calling themselves group work agencies. Braucher himself favored the title, education-recreation work.

Group work was in a time of transition, leaving old friends, making new ones. It still remembered what it had learned from progressive education, especially the importance of democracy in group learning, and what recreation had taught it, the benefits of play, but it wanted to apply the principles of education to its own craft and had grown weary of "wigwagging for the sake of merit badges."[37] At the university level, group workers found friends among the social scientists. Social psychology was not yet firmly established as a respectable discipline, but sociology and psychology were combining and those who knew a bit of both were to teach group work a most valuable technique—how to change groups.

In 1930 Wilber I. Newstetter's study of a group of boys at camp confined itself almost exclusively to data bearing on group acceptability, i.e., the group's acceptance of the individual, and the individual's acceptance of the group. Of immediate interest to the group worker was the study's attempt to explore the possibility of changing group life in accordance with formulated objectives.[38]

The small group, cohesion, and individual adjustment became matters for empirical research; evaluation took on a new hard meaning. Such study called for men with a grasp of the scientific method and with the proper tools, such as sociometrics. It was natural that group work should turn to universities and research organizations for help. The Boston Federation of Neighborhood Houses formed a committee to plan study and research, relying heavily on university professors and researchers. The proposed study's objective was to discover and test methods that would measure program evolution, the effect of the group on the individual, and group leadership.[39] In studying the small club as a distinctive kind of group, attention was focused upon (1) its unique features as a social unit; (2) the special values that the small group could afford its members; and lastly, but of great importance, (3) the adult leader's part in realizing these values.

In Detroit a research project of the National Youth Administration originated from a joint request by Franklin Street Settlement and the Merrill-Palmer Institute for aid in studying the settlement's boys' work program. Fourteen clubs were studied and 227 club members repeatedly tested—in all, there were 926 individual tests administered. The report was one of the first systematic attempts to evaluate by means of objective criteria the results of group work and the efforts of group leaders.[40]

The implications of this type of research were not lost on group workers. Clearly the group leader was more than an exemplar of democracy, a teacher, an advisor; he was, in addition, a change agent who could deliberately manipulate the group. The group itself was an instrument of change. In the late 1930s, as group work drew further away from informal education, there was considerable deliberation on the means of altering "classes" or "teams" so that they might become "groups."[41]

Group work was still uncertain what it was. In 1935 Newstetter defined group work as an educational process emphasizing: (1) the development and social adjustment of an individual through voluntary group membership; (2) the use of the association as a means of furthering other socially desirable ends.[42] It was concerned with both individual growth and social betterment. The combination of these objectives was the distinguishing mark of group work "as a process." The next year the American Association for the Study of Group Work was founded. Its membership including volunteers as well as employed workers, for there were no limits on eligibility. Group work's relation to the field of social work was still tenuous, since group workers were not sure whether they actually formed a profession separate from social work. The National Conference of Social Work, which treated group work as a separate subject until 1939, reflected this ambiguity. The aims of AASGW, "to clarify and refine both the philosophy and the practice of group work," were difficult to attain.[43] For one thing, many felt that group work was primarily a method of informal education. Grace Coyle had no doubt that group work was part of social work, but that it had one foot in education made its function "more largely educational than therapeutic and for that reason it should be classed as one aspect of the progressive education movement."[44] Informal education was intertwined with notions of democracy, so that as late as 1939, Charles Hendry could write that group work "has no objectives of its own except in the sense that by its very nature it derives both its meaning and motivation from democracy."[45]

Group work's main dilemma, however, stemmed not from its inability to define itself or to discover its own methods and techniques but from the fact that its chief instrument of intervention, the group, was not really in the hands of the professional. Group leaders were volunteers, largely untrained and often unskilled. How was group work to prove itself? The proposals were many: that professionals help in the recruiting and selection of volunteers, that professionals train volunteers, that they supervise volunteers. These tasks generally meant that professionals stayed in administrative positions and had comparatively little to do with the actual direction of groups. Yet even here was a flaw: relatively few agency staff members were trained in group work; and their interest in further education was slight.

The Group Leaders

The manpower shortage in the fields of recreation and adult education during the depression, caused by increased demands for service and the inability of organizations to hire more workers, meant that staffs in group work agencies were subject to an additional strain that they could not bear alone. Agency executives urged their professionals to share the work with lay committees and service volunteers. The Emergency Relief Appropriations Act in 1935 benefited group work agencies through the Works Progress Administration, later (in 1939) to be named the Works Projects Administration. Although originally it was hoped that private industry and WPA together would be able to absorb most of the unemployed, it soon became apparent that WPA would have to supply the jobs. WPA's objective was to employ 3,500,000 people on relief. Since Congress excluded certain types of projects such as slum clearance, demolition work, and military production for fear of competing with private industry, the health, welfare, and cultural organizations absorbed a large proportion of the WPA workers. The Federal Emergency Relief Administration had already opened the way for the employment of emergency workers in the field of recreation and adult education,[46] but FERA had been set up as a temporary measure, and its programs were not as far-reaching as those of WPA. WPA projects included home crafts, housekeeping aides, recreation, library work, music, art, workers' education. Much of this work was done with the aid and assistance of lay advisory committees.[47] These committees worked with existing agencies and organizations, such as settlements, the Ys, churches, and clubs.

83

Eduard C. Lindeman was director of the WPA recreation division as well as planning consultant to WPA's professional and service division. His commitment to recreation was firm, and he believed in making recreation a profession with trained and competent leaders. But agencies, which supported federal work relief in principle, often opposed WPA. Settlements, in particular, were slow to cooperate with WPA, and government officials found them difficult to deal with. A 1938 survey of settlements in ten cities showed that a number of houses had decided that it was no longer profitable to use WPA workers and that the time had come "to build up a staff that can maintain a high quality of service, and again develop a body of volunteers from the community to augment their number."[48] Staff members complained that WPA workers, who had replaced staff members and volunteers in many instances, were inefficient. According to the survey report, WPA had functioned best where the staff "had been of such a number and quality that it could take on the training and supervision of WPA and NYA workers without too much strain."[49] How far these were unbiased judgments is impossible to say; industry was not the only sector that feared competition from federal workers.

Volunteers posed less of a threat to regular staff in group work agencies than did emergency workers. These volunteers served as specialists—teachers, craftsmen, physical education instructors—and as leaders of clubs and interest groups. As has been noted, the division of volunteers into the categories of specialists and group leaders was common in some agencies—the settlements, the YMCA, and the YWCA. Other organizations, e.g., the Scouts, did not use the distinction very much. The mastery of certain rituals and skills—knots and what nots—was expected of most Scout leaders. Still other associations such as the 4-H Clubs for farm youth or the Junior Audubon Club, a wild life society, required a specialized knowledge of all their leaders or at least a willingness to become skilled.

The evaluation of specialists presented a problem to group work executives. Agencies prized supervision as the prerogative of professionals and many placement bureaus demanded that volunteers be supervised. But the appraisal of competence, a necessary part of the supervision of specialists, was outside the ability of many group work directors. A study of program volunteers or specialists in 84 YWCAs in the mid-1930s highlighted the problem, but the report failed to come up with any recommendations that offered a genuine solution.[50]

Where there were well-established programs with their own trained and skilled directors, the problem of evaluation was not so acute. The YMCA, for instance, had an extensive physical health and education program. In 1935 the association had 626 physical and health education specialists. The persons enrolled in these activities were 43.3 percent of all those enrolled in every kind of group activity.[51] In the 1930s studies were conducted to arrive at a critical evaluation of volunteer physical education programs for the purpose of establishing policies and standards.[52] Outside the broad field of group work, such empirical studies of volunteer programs were rare. The plan for conducting the YMCA study involved a committee of four who worked out what seemed to be important items in standards and policies of a lay leadership program. The list was sent out to forty-two experienced physical directors who were especially interested in lay leadership, with instructions to grade each item on a five-point scale ranging from "essential" to "no value." The results of their evaluation were then tabulated and analyzed.[53] The composite opinion of the forty-two specialists became an instrument or measure for evaluating local programs. The purpose of this device was to help each local physical director analyze his methods of using lay leaders by comparing his practice with the composite opinion of the specialists who had carefully graded each item of practice. It was hoped by means of this device: (1) to show the local director how his practice was at variance with the composite opinion of specialists experienced in lay leadership; and (2) to stimulate improvement in practice. A central commission offered its services to local directors who, having evaluated their own practice, requested assistance in improving their lay leadership programs.

The YMCA conducted studies on the attendance, occupations, nationality, church affiliation, motivation, supervision, budget costs, service, and turnover of volunteers. Perhaps the most daring research was that which the South Chicago YMCA conducted on comparative efficiency of volunteers and staff. The research attempted to compare the teaching effectiveness of paid and unpaid workers over a period of four years, beginning in 1930. The first part of the research focused on the teaching of elementary skills in learn-to-swim courses. No significant differences were found in the effectiveness of the volunteers and staff members. Nonetheless, the results were inconclusive if one takes into account the contamination factor in the research. Staff members trained and supervised volunteers, and so presumably contributed to the volunteers' success. The results of the study might have indicated, however, that given training and supervision, volunteers were as effective as staff in teaching elementary skills.[54] The second part of the research on the effectiveness of volunteers and staff in teaching highly specialized skills—gymnastics, competitive swimming, wrestling, boxing, tumbling, basketball—is open to question in the choice of criteria.[55] The criterion of effectiveness was the number of city or state titles that the various teams won, but —as everyone realized in his or her calmer moments—the coach is not always to blame when the team loses.

Despite the ubiquity of the specialist or program volunteer, social work's professional interest was centered mainly on the group leader of the common or garden variety. The group without a prefix was, after all, social work's raw material from which it hoped to build a new specialty. When social group workers referred to groups they frequently had in mind clubs "with a free type of program, definite internal organization, and a large degree of self-determination of what is done."[56] When the term was so used to signify a club, it excluded the systematic class method predominating in certain physical educational and religious activities, as well as "mass recreation" in parks and playgrounds. Club or group leaders were distinguished from volunteer activity assistants, counselors, interviewers, instructors, coaches, office helpers, supervisors, and committee members.

From a sample of group records it is possible to reconstruct the club of the 1930s. The National Federation of Settlements formed a Committee on the Study of the Records of Groups and collected actual group records. In addition, the committee, which was most active in the early 1930s, produced models and outlines of records for the assistance of group leaders, so that the tasks of these volunteers are delineated for us. The collection is poorly annotated, making it impossible to ascertain who wrote the various records, but the picture of club life is nonetheless valuable.

The settlement club was free to choose its own name and activity. The Who's Who of Clubs included names that ripped—the Iroquois, Cardinals, Amicos, Zonta—names that danced—Jolly Janes, Red Ravens, Moths, Full of Fun—and names that meant business—Model Airplane, Woodcraft, Dramatics, Almost Everything. In St. Paul, out of affection for a volunteer group leader, a bunch of Italian boys, aged seven to nine, chose to be known as "The O'Hallorans." The charter members were hardly Irish—Fred Gatto, Joe Arrigone, John Policano, Albert Capocassa, Ralph Cuciarrella, Dominick Cotroneo. But if the members were full of fun, their leaders were in earnest. So the records show. The task of the leader was to explore the characteristics and needs of the group; to understand individuals and their needs; to use leadership techniques wisely and with care; and, through outside contacts, to estimate the effects of environmental factors on the group. The leader was responsible for planning meetings with the group and kept account of attendance.

Although the leader was a man of strategy, the technique of good leadership required that he act in a democratic fashion, when possible; that he suggest rather than demand. "L (leader) asked them if they wished to put on a stunt for Stunt Night. They all agreed that they would like to. L. suggested a few stunts and the rest of the evening was spent in planning and going over the stunts."[57]

The model reports written for volunteers or students tended to be more diagnostic—and profuse—than actual club records. The records of Model Airplane, a club of a dozen boys in Cleveland's East End Neighborhood House, are extant from October 1, 1931, to February 2, 1932. The business of the club was building model planes, as succinctly recorded:[58]

28 January 1932: 7 present, 2 absent.
Julius T. called the meeting to order at 7:45.
The boys discussed what models they had decided to build, several have decided to build a small commercial model designed by Mr. B. [the leader]. Others were building Fokker D7 and D8 models. One was going to build a Lockheed Vega. Chester L. gave a short talk on wing construction in relation to the fuselage. Following this, estimates of materials were drawn up, and prices were placed on materials necessary.
The boys wanted to invest in a model aircraft magazine but when Mr. B. told them the price they had to give it up as too high.
Meeting closed and next meeting was planned for the 28th.

An earlier meeting which provided ample opportunity for a discussion on democracy, conflict situations, treatment, interpretation and procedure, received even less coverage:[59]

87

Special Meeting, December 28, 1931: 7 present, 5 absent.
Members took entire responsibility of meeting and conducted (it) themselves. Voted to meet 4 nights a week. John L., George F., and Joe L.,
Louis B., took the greatest interest. Decided on a meeting Jan. 11. Julius
T. is a decidedly good leader and is responsible. However, he rules with
an iron hand. Joe L. rebelled a little as he believed each could act on his
own initiative in building. Others felt a rigid program should be followed. Next meeting was called for Jan. 5, 1932.

Social work found the appraisal of group leaders a most elusive
task. At a round-table discussion in Philadelphia in 1932 "the over-
whelming testimony" of those present was to the effect that "no
recognized standards are set up for volunteer leaders to achieve."[60]
A commission of AASGW, some seven years later, acknowledged that
few group work agencies evaluated their leaders. Where appraisal
was attempted—notably in a small number of YMCAs—the leader's
qualities and characteristics were rated on a scale or were recorded
in a written commentary. The commission proposed that agencies
should evaluate their group leaders on their qualifications, relationships, administrative ability, and leadership techniques. Qualifications referred to personal talents, an understanding of the philosophy
and function of the agency, definiteness of the leader's aims, and the
ability to plan.

The commission listed leadership techniques at length. The
adequacy of group leadership was measured by the leader's ability
to use the group activity "to stimulate desirable social habits; to use
the club to provide experience in the democratic process and to
supply the opportunity for positive action for social betterment."
Democracy, socialization, social action: each thread joined group
work with its past. There was, during this period, little effort to
separate these three traditions, or to establish priorities. The techniques of leadership also included skill in stimulating the members'
participation in the club program, interclub activities and in house
projects. Each of these techniques was pertinent to group leadership;
their diversity, however, reflected a variety of goals not necessarily
incompatible but scattered nonetheless. Group work had not yet
defined its objectives clearly.

Selection, Training, and Supervision

Heading a list of methods for discovering volunteers, a YMCA manual had this item: "Someone volunteers." But group work agencies could not rely on offers of service, however uncomplicated this might have been, and most of them used additional means of recruitment—public addresses, newspaper advertisements, orientation courses, college contacts, and special committees. Normally, group work agencies, in contrast to casework agencies, did their own recruiting. They made comparatively little use of placement bureaus, although among smaller agencies this method was not unknown.

Another feature of group work recruitment was its lay character. Agencies such as the Boys' Clubs of America used their staff along with laymen to recruit volunteers, but the more common procedure was to rely almost entirely on laymen in the community, service volunteers, and board members to enlist new helpers. Agencies felt laymen could provide a continuity of contact with the community and were in a better position to recruit leaders indigenous to the neighborhood. This was also a way of extending the influence of the agency beyond its walls and brought the organization to the attention of community leaders. Lastly, since the depression had increased greatly the administrative duties of staff members, these could not be expected to undertake active recruitment in addition to their training and supervisory responsibilities. Staff members were willing to act as resource persons, advising the lay recruiters, but they avoided direct involvement.

The training of leaders was common in group work agencies, but it was not universal. Two camps existed. There were those who dreaded seeing skill in group work being taught "lest it become coldly intellectual" and those who favored "the gathering of a professional body of knowledge." The advocates of training said that instruction was an aid and not an obstacle to "the good heart," and that "light and warmth can both be realized when feeling and intelligence together go into an undertaking."[61] The "extreme reliance" upon volunteers would hurt group work unless there was a corresponding emphasis on training.

In 1939 Helen Fudge, in a study of girls' clubs, found that about half of the national nonsectarian organizations that had leisure, recreation, and special interest groups reported a comprehensive training program (courses, conferences, institutes, etc.) available for group leaders. In addition, out of twenty-four organizations that submitted data, twenty-two offered publications in the form of informational pamphlets, instructions, handbooks, manuals, and textbooks. Nineteen organizations had official organs, and one organization used local newspapers as a means of supplying information on various topics.

Apart from publications, courses, institutes, and in-service training were common. Lecture courses were modeled after education in professional schools. For the most part they were orientation courses dealing with the theory of group work. The Detroit Commission for the Study of Work conducted a group work leaders' institute that consisted of thirteen weekly sessions and was attended by a selected number of the city's volunteer club leaders. The course provided basic data on the local population. Speakers lectured on the psychological basis of leisure-time interests, theories of progressive education, the teaching of creative art, community resources, and group records. The trainees visited various clubs to see the application of theory to practice. In settlement houses, preliminary training included the teaching of skills. There was actual practice in games, songs, stunts, crafts, stories, and "anything else that will give a new leader skills with which to get started."[62] Courses that provided practice in group activities were not departing from the professional education of schools of social work. Professional schools had lessons in dramatics, music, crafts, dancing, and group games.

Continuing education for volunteer leaders was a feature of the scouting movement. The national organization of the Girl Scouts did not require training of its leaders, but it urged and offered a comprehensive training program arranged progressively. A general course, outlining the Girl Scouts' program as a whole, provided basic training. In addition there were courses planned for leaders with specific needs—a course for troop leaders who required training in outdoor work, a course in camping, a special activities course, and an advanced course in scouting. Volunteer training in the Boy Scouts, which increased in volume at the outset of the depression, was extensive and well-organized. Scouts, with a motto for every occasion, believed that "Every Scouter should be trained for his job." In the early 1930s, responding to demands from the field for a higher level of training, the Scouts' Education Service developed a five-year progressive training program for scoutmasters, leading to the high honor awards—the Scoutmaster's Key and the Scouter's Training

Award—emblems of achievement among scoutmasters comparable to the Eagle Scout Badge among Scouts. The program included courses in the elements of scout leadership, troop administration, the principles of first aid, specialization courses, camping, and reading. Experience in the field was part of the training program. The scoutmaster, upon completion of each intermediate phase of the five-year program, earned an advanced certificate. No single organization approached the Boy Scouts of America in the thoroughness and breadth of its training program.[63]

Field experience and in-service training were characteristic of group work agencies. Apprenticeship had a longer history than formal instruction in youth-serving agencies, and it was particularly suited to organizations, such as the Ys and settlements, with specialized programs. In-service training appealed to many social workers who favored teaching as they were taught—by "getting into the situation and absorbing the theory as the work goes on."[64] To be successful, in-service training required supervision, conferences, and direction; but these were not always provided. In the YMCA, Leaders' Councils met regularly to insure their own guidance. They devoted meetings to the discussion of problems that arose in the course of their work as group leaders. Sometimes these discussions were carried on around general themes such as character education, creative leadership, club programs, and the like.

The fact that few professionals were group leaders put the burden of advancing the cause of group work on the shoulders of supervisors. Arthur Swift, in an address before the New York State Conference of Social Work in 1935, pleaded for more and better supervision to make up for the deficiencies of volunteers.[65] Lloyd McClow, a YMCA executive, declared supervision to be "the weakest link in the chain."[66] Settlement leaders had similar complaints and pleas. Praising the tradition of volunteer participation in group work, Charles Hendry of Boys' Clubs of America warned the 1940 National Conference of Social Work, "The successful use of volunteer personnel . . . depends in large measure upon the ratio which obtains between professional supervision and volunteer leadership. This ratio includes the factor of quality as well as the factor of quantity."[67]

The group supervisor, of course, was not a simple type or kind: he could be anybody from an activities secretary in the Y to a director in a community center or, in a few instances, a volunteer. The excellence of supervision depended upon each organization, and opinions regarding adequacy differed. "It is surprising to find," wrote Ellen Geer in 1933, "that group work, such as club leadership in settlement houses, which attracts many volunteers, has lagged behind in accepting the importance of adequate training, though for many years a few leading settlement houses have had staff members for the supervision of their volunteers."[68] Asked to comment on the statement while still in manuscript form, Albert Kennedy, "Mr. Settlement" himself, was unlikely to take kindly to criticism of neighborhood houses and went on the defensive. He wrote, "Mrs. Geer's statement is probably accurate, but its color looks a little peculiar to me. The fact of the matter is that practically all staff members in settlements, with the exception of teachers and in some degree they are not exempt, are supervisors of volunteers. One pays directors of boys' and girls' work, etc., first to know their groups and second to train and supervise the work of volunteers."[69]

The supervisor generally attended some meetings to observe and evaluate the performance of group leaders. He tried to act as an invisible guest, his aim being, "so to conduct himself as to keep the situation as nearly as possible as it would have been had he not been present."[70] The professional group worker in his honest moments could admit that his presence as supervisor seldom went unnoticed, but in the workaday world supervision was the professional's only real link with live groups.

Summary

When *The Group*, the official journal of the American Association for the Study of Group Work, was started in February 1939, the subtitle of the bulletin, *in Education-Recreation-Social Work*, described a certain unity of interest. But no amount of hyphenating could quite resolve the tension of that particular triangle. Traditions, or at least elements of tradition, were common to all three movements, but differences were apparent. Where did social group work belong? Social group work had not yet realized that it could become something that was neither progressive education nor recreation. The definition of its most fundamental concept, the group itself, was still vague. The clustering of recreation groups, classes, and clubs under the one group work umbrella was usual. It explains among other things why some of the major youth-serving organizations such as the Boy Scouts of America, which later went their separate ways, were during this period at home among the other group work agencies.

As group work agencies had different goals, so too they used their volunteers in various ways. Program volunteers generally served in classes or groups interested in drama, music, art, housekeeping, or physical education, where a specialization was required of the instructor. When skill was not the main objective, volunteers served as group or club leaders. It was easier to define some groups than others. A scout troop, for instance, had its written code and regulations; and consequently in the scouting movement, manuals could spell out precisely the leader's responsibility. In the settlements or in the Ys, on the other hand, the definition of a group was more difficult. However, since professional interest focused on the leisure-time club, a body of literature grew up that delineated the duties of group leaders.

The name, group leader, was itself misleading. It did not imply an indigenous leader, even though groups frequently elected one of their own members to direct their activity. The leader had a dual obligation to the agency and the group. A link between the two, he served as a resource person for the group and as a means of agency control. The leader was not an autocrat, however; he was much more a group advisor who maintained discipline when necessary and who helped the members achieve common, stated objectives.

Volunteer group leadership presented a challenge to organized social work. The professional group worker's actual contact with groups was slight in comparison to the volunteer's. What control the professional exercised and what service he rendered had to come from his position as administrator, teacher, supervisor and, occasionally, researcher. If now and then he was uneasy with amateur efforts in the field, he was sensible enough to realize that without the volunteer there could be no group work. As a result, the volunteer received attention, training, supervision, and encouragement to carry on.

• • •

CHAPTER 6

Citizen Participation

• • •

The Politics of Planning

The aspirations of an age are best recognized in its clichés. Phrases such as citizen participation, lay leadership, and grass-root democracy attracted men and women at the very time when social engineering, central planning, and national control were in vogue. Tradition sanctified citizen participation, but there was another element that made many Americans rebel against expert and bureaucrat alike —the prospect of a planned society. There were two nations in the womb—Esau, the hunter and man of the fields, and his brother Jacob, the schemer. Americans were aware of the dialectic of this allegory, and at stake was a heritage. "In the Epilogue the dreams of those who saw Utopia are shattered and people find they are marching backwards towards the Middle Ages—as regimented man," warned Herbert Hoover, the most articulate spokesman for the oldtime religion.[1] What matter if the yeoman farmer was a myth, as Richard Hofstadter has demonstrated, or if the business entrepreneur was not wholly innocent. As Hoover saw it, "God-fearing men and women of honesty whose stamina and character and fearless assertion of rights led them to make their own way in life" were being forgotten, and in their place had come bureaucrats and "those amateur sociologists" who were misleading the nation. Hoover, with a romantic's love for capital letters, championed Liberty against Regimentation. Like Reinhold Niebuhr whose eschatology pitted the children of light against the children of darkness, Hoover, the polemicist, separated the good from the bad. But as a politician in a world where even the angels are tarnished, he found it more difficult to devise a means whereby the good might prosper. In truth, he was caught up in the debate of the decade—how to plan prosperity while maintaining freedom. Despite the accusations of his enemies, Hoover was not wedded to the theory of laissez faire which he considered outmoded, but his principles forced him to espouse maximum individual effort and minimum government intervention. Theoretically, his philosophy was not opposed to national planning, but the strong emphasis on neighborliness made bureaucracy seem less important.

Hoover leaned heavily on good will and voluntary endeavor to put things right. The President's Emergency Committee for Employment and its successor, the President's Organization on Unemployment Relief, summoned local businessmen and voluntary associations to play a mighty role in bringing back prosperity. In retrospect, few would question the idealism of Hoover who tried to fight the depression with volunteers instead of a professional welfare army, but his tactics were ill-suited to the times. Even the Reconstruction Finance Corporation was little more, in his eyes, than a government supplement to citizen self-help.

Roosevelt did not repudiate Hoover's doctrine of citizen involvement (he would not have dared), but he changed the context of participation. He was committed to national planning in a way that Hoover was not, and though members of his administration might have differed in their choice of methods, few doubted the necessity of overhead control. The National Recovery Administration and the Agricultural Adjustment Administration were pledges of the government's willingness to intervene in industry and farming. The Social Security Act of 1935 went further in making economic security, even individual security, the concern of the federal government. Only within the firm limits of national planning and control did the Roosevelt administration encourage grass-root democracy, but within this context it was eager to proclaim itself champion of the common man. It sought ways and means to foster citizen participation.

Organized social work was equally set on national planning. In round upon round of congressional hearings, from 1930 onward, social workers made the profession's position quite clear: social workers wanted federal control in matters of economic security. The 1934 National Conference through its principal speakers, Mary van Kleeck and Eduard Lindeman, adopted a radical stance in demanding a fight against economic privilege.[2] But the profession's dedication to central authority and overhead planning meant the ascendancy of the social welfare administrator. Organized social work perceived the danger of excluding the public from public affairs. The profession had two standard devices, learned over the years in the field of administration and community organization, for involving citizens in welfare—the use of boards and what people later came to call indigenous leadership.

Most social work writers glorified boards in an effort to insure citizen participation or to demonstrate the effectiveness of lay leadership. Yet, at times, a note of despair crept into their discussions as though they feared they might be defending a legal fiction. There was some recognition that the existence of boards did not necessarily guarantee democracy. Some organizations, notably the YMCA, were fearful that they were merely perpetuating an oligarchy through their board representation. The "art of conferencing" was also used to widen participation, often in a genuine attempt to give everyone a voice, occasionally simply as a palliative. Conferences, workshops, meetings, advisory committees were established for the purpose of involving a large circle of citizens in social welfare. But critics gave discussion a low rating. The acid remark of Saul Alinsky that community organization was too often paper organization found favor among those social workers who believed that social welfare was in danger of becoming an autocratic system no longer controlled by the citizens of the country.[3]

Public welfare, in particular, seemed open to the charge of autocracy, since it was here that two establishments—the government and the social work profession—joined forces.

Public Welfare Boards and Committees

Pierce Atwater, who lectured on administration at the Universities of Minnesota and Chicago during the 1930s, believed that lay "boards of authority" were unpopular because they conflicted with academic concepts of democracy.[4] But more than concepts of democracy impeded the use of boards; the laws of the land, state, or county also determined the shape of administration. In federal government, paid administrative boards or commissions were established, and legal requirements limited the function of these boards. At the state and local level, boards were common, but they had various functions according to the laws and by-laws governing the different agencies. A review of state public welfare laws in effect in 1940 showed that 47 states had 53 state boards that either advised or directed the executive in carrying out the duties of his office. However, the board members were not always volunteers. In 28 states, board members were reimbursed for expenses only; in 17 states provision was made for expenses plus a small honorarium; in four states there was no legal provision for payment. Local board members seldom, if ever, received salaries, though reimbursement of expenses was common.[5]

The law, too, determined the kind of the responsibilities that public welfare boards carried. State and county boards had heavy administrative duties, as is shown by Table 6 by Helen Martz in her study of the nature of responsibilities which the law assigned to these boards in 1940.[6]

TABLE 4

Nature of Responsibilities Assigned by Law to State
and Local Boards of Public Welfare, 1940

Function	Number of States in Which Functions Were Assigned to	
	State Board	Local Board
Establish minimum qualifications for personnel	23	1
Establish standards of performance	12	2
Set salary scales	22	10
Appoint director	27	17
Appoint other staff	16	16
Approve director's staff appointments	7	7
Make decisions of eligibility for assistance in individual cases	7	13
Determine policies, rules, and regulations	41	11

Although there were minor variations, two forms of organization were most commonly found in state, county, and city public welfare agencies. The first type followed the departmental or cabinet plan, under which a paid director headed the agency but was responsible to the official or group by whom he was appointed. In this type of organization, the director of the department frequently had an unpaid advisory committee of citizens to whom he turned (or did not turn) for advice. The second type of organization had a citizen's administrative board and a paid executive. Where this second plan was followed, the primary responsibility for the direction of the department belonged to the administrative or governing board of citizens, often five or seven in number. The board members were usually appointed with overlapping terms so as to give them a greater possibility of independence from any one appointing official. Theoreticians debated the merits of each system. Writers such as Atwater and Arthur Dunham[7] favored citizen committees, because this kind of arrangement tended to prevent political interference in the work of the department and provided lay participation in public social welfare. Those who opposed citizen "boards of authority" argued that the boards violated the principles of unified governmental responsibility by placing an intermediary between the chief executive authority of the city or county and the department head. In New York the majority of members of the Governor's Commission on Unemployment Relief took this latter view in their report of 1935.[8] The majority made the recommendation that a commission be appointed by the governor and be responsible to him, that the board be reduced in size, and have its powers changed to include the following: determination of broad questions of policy, establishment of rules and regulations, service as a board of review, and service as an advisory body to the Commissioner of Social Welfare.[9]

The recommendations of the New York Governor's Commission seem to verify Atwater's assertion that many felt that the exercise of wide powers should be vested only in elected officials—a point of view that Atwater did not share. Furthermore, state legislatures, city councils, and county boards disliked conferring upon appointive nonpaid boards wide powers to control expenditures for public welfare. On one point there was general agreement: even where citizen boards existed, they should not have many executive duties. Boards serving as multiheaded executives were unpopular, since they appeared to be inefficient substitutes for a single competent executive directly responsible for agency operations.

One way in which citizen participation was fostered and at the same time kept in its place was through the formation of advisory boards. Sincere or cynical administrators used these boards at national, state, and local levels. Advisory boards were not new in federal government, but they multiplied during Roosevelt's presidency. The New Deal had a philosophy of citizen advice which, apart from other advantages, was useful in countering accusations of regimentation. Citizen participation was all but written into the National Recovery Act. In setting up FERA and CWA, Roosevelt insisted that they should have advisory committees, and the pattern was followed in other agencies and projects.

The National Youth Administration (NYA), created by executive order on June 26, 1935, was among the federal agencies that made most use of advisory boards. The task of NYA was to extend the college aid plan, already in existence, to include needy high school children. It also established three other programs: part-time work for out-of-school and out-of-work youth in families on relief, concurrent training, and the encouragement of constructive leisure-time activity for these young people, and vocational guidance and placement for all unemployed youth. When establishing NYA, Roosevelt created a National Advisory Committee, headed by Charles Taussig, which was responsible to the president. From that time forward, the National Advisory Committee met and reported regularly to Roosevelt, and to the administrator of NYA, Aubrey Williams. State and local advisory committees corresponded to state, district, and county NYA organizations. By 1936 all the states, with the exception of South Dakota, had advisory committees—a total membership of 532, of which 433 were men and 99 women.[10] Two years later there were more than 2,600 local committees.[11]

The director of the National Advisory Committee for most of its existence was S. Burns Weston. He acted as assistant to the chairman and served in a liaison capacity between the National Advisory Committee and the administrator of NYA. Weston was typical of that school of New Deal administrators who were wary of centralized administration. He preferred to act as mediator, ever ready to conciliate, and to compromise where necessary. His philosophy is summed up in a communication to John Binns, state administrator in Washington:[12]

There are two basic factors from which we are endeavoring to project our thinking. The first is the importance of decentralizing to the local level recognition of individual and community responsibility, in regard to the many questions with which the federal government is dealing on a national basis. This is especially necessary if . . . we are to prevent the local community from assuming the early attitude of letting Uncle Sam do it. The second factor is perhaps more a matter of technique;

to wit, encouragement not only of adults, but of youth itself, to participate in the advisory committee sphere of action.

Political sense was necessary in dealing with state administrators,
many of whom were suspicious of citizen advisory boards. Weston
was careful not to force his programs on the states. But caution had
its price. A study of the organization, membership, and activities of
local and state advisory committees for 1938–40 brought to light
serious defects.[13] In 1939–40 the state committees, which varied in
size from five persons in Colorado to 45 in Maine, showed no particular relation to the size or population of the states. Eighteen states
(slightly over 38 percent of the number reporting) did not hold a
single meeting of their advisory committees during the year. Eleven
committees met only once, while the remaining eighteen committees met from two to twelve times. The study report explained the
inactivity of the state committees, "[It] shows that either the groups
have no clear understanding of their functions or duties or the established objectives have been outgrown and discarded, leaving the
committees with little to do." The report did not refer to the indifference of state administrators, although Washington believed that this
was a relevant factor.

The 1940 study provided important information on the membership of the state advisory committees. Essentially the study comprised three surveys: one covered the period 1938–39; the second,
1939–40; the third, a special survey, was conducted six months after
the 1939–40 survey but in the same year. Table 5 is a summary of the
surveys' total membership and representation.[14]

TABLE 5

*State NYA Advisory Committees: Membership
and Representation, 1938–40*

	Total Members	Edu-cation	Busi-ness	Labor	Agri-culture	Youth	Negro	Other
1938–39	733	180	96	65	64	85	65	178
1939–40	820	198	113	78	71	75	49	213
Special Survey	811	218	122	80	66	75	46	204

When the state advisory committees were first set up, it was
recommended that broad representative committees should reflect
a cross-section of community interests. The recommendation was
that members should represent the interests of education, labor,

100

business, agriculture, minority groups, and the like. Not all these groups existed in every community so that some departures from these classifications were allowable. By and large, the concept of broad representation was accepted as the standard. The special survey pointed up certain significant trends. There was a tendency to increase representation of the education group, in spite of the fact that in the majority of cases education was already most prominent. The report recommended that business representation and labor representation (which had remained fairly static) be increased. Agricultural representation was low, but this was of less importance than deficiencies in labor and youth, since in many highly industrialized areas the value of agricultural representation was questionable. Youth representation had declined. The responses did not indicate why this was so. The responses did suggest, however, that in many instances the youth representatives were among the most inarticulate and inactive members of the committees. In some instances, the survey showed that members who were designated as "Youth" were neither young nor connected with youth organizations, but adults from youth-serving agencies or individuals interested in youth welfare. Representation of the Negro group had declined according to figures tabulated from the survey, but there was some doubt regarding these figures, since not all reports clearly marked their Negro members. The group designated as "Others" formed the second largest group. The report did not state how this group was made up, but it supplied the criteria for "good selections of representation." These included: persons from prominent women's organizations that provided a valuable medium of public contact; persons from youth-serving agencies so as to supply coordination of youth activities; prominent members of the medical, dental, or health associations, for the expansion of health services to young people; and state agents of general education board.

In considering local advisory committees, the report noted that many of the observations concerning the degree of representation in state advisory committees applied equally to local committees. Education was most prominently represented; business, especially industry, had a smaller representation; labor was poorly represented; youth, agriculture, and Negroes were small minorities, while the miscellaneous group was a new category—local public officials. In some instances, city councilmen made up the entire committee. In general, as might be expected of small homogeneous communities, there was less variety in representation. There was a tendency, too, to organize functional or specialized committees to meet specific ends. A summary of the total number of committees, the types of committees (general, specialized, or both), total membership and youth membership is shown in Table 6.[15]

TABLE 6

Membership of Local NYA Advisory Committees,
1938–40

	Total Committees	Specialized	General	Spec. & General	No. of Members	No. of Youth
1938–39	3,013				18,321	3,491
1939–40	3,356	1,026	2,310	20	19,610	2,270
Special Survey	1,864	90	1,772	2	12,839	334

The total number of local committees decreased drastically within the year 1939–40, as the special survey showed. This probably relates to a general decline in the use of committees, but the use of vastly different methods of data collection provides an additional explanation for the variation. There is some probability that the estimates of previous years had been too generous. While the total number of committees decreased by almost 50 percent, the total number of members only decreased by some 30 percent, indicating an increase in the size of some committees. It must also be noted that "Youth" had a more precise definition in the special survey, and this accounts in a large measure for the sudden drop in numbers. Still, the figure remains indicative of the small part young people played in local advisory work.

What was the function of state and local committees? To say that it was to advise administrators would be to minimize the committees' actual work. Certainly, the committees had no administrative duties —these were the responsibility of NYA administrators, but the committees achieved some success in aiding NYA programs, especially in school and community public relations, in establishing and furthering health programs, employment services, youth training, and in social action. As World War II approached, NYA tried to coordinate its operations with the national defense program. The advisory committees were asked to help in drafting projects and in coordinating plans for expanding health services, defense training, housing, and facilities, and in the development of human resources and skills. In 1940 Massachusetts and Kansas held state advisory meetings devoted to a discussion of defense needs; Florida and New York established cross-representation with state defense councils. The following year national, state, and local advisory committees engaged in extensive research on the nonmilitary aspects of national defense, such as health, housing, recreation, and education.

Boards in Private Agencies

In many private agencies board service was the major medium of volunteer participation in social welfare. Theoretically, boards determined agency policy, using committees and staff consultation as a means to this end. In 1935 the Family Welfare Association of America, in studying the qualifications of board members, analyzed the replies to questionnaires sent to boards and staffs in 179 private and 11 public agencies. An analysis of the responses suggested that board members and staffs considered boards responsible for:[16]

1. The effectiveness of the agency in meeting the needs of those people in the community for which the agency had accepted responsibility.
2. Determining and supporting the policies and practice of the agency.
3. Initiating, modifying, or expanding the practice of the agency in the light of the changing needs of the community.
4. Interpreting the needs and attitudes of the community to the staff; and interpreting the work of the agency to the community with the objective of getting both social and financial support.

The report made little distinction between boards in public and private agencies, although their functions were normally different.

The organizational structure of a private agency generally consisted of a governing board (which was the group of ultimate control), an executive, and staff. While an organization's charter, constitution, or by-laws might give control to the organization's contributors or members, the board usually exercised authority. Some agencies had self-perpetuating boards; others made provision for the election of boards, frequently at the annual meeting of members. In settlement houses the power and function of boards varied somewhat depending on whether the settlement was a limited corporation, a membership agency, or an auxiliary of another organization. Except where the settlement was an auxiliary body, the board either assumed direct responsibility for finance, management, and control or else delegated the function to a small group of its own number. Jay A. Urice of the YMCA asserted that the layman's legal control of an association was a prerequisite for good lay-staff relations.[17] Urice borrowed from Arthur Swift, director of a New York YMCA survey, when he proposed a classification of functions that differentiated the tasks of laymen from those of professionals. Policy determination was the responsibility of laymen alone. The responsibility derived from their legal status and their relationship to the community. In Urice's opinion, laymen and professionals together were responsible for policy formulation. This demanded cooperation, each party bringing particular insights, experience, and skill to bear on the problems involved. Lastly, policy execution was the chief business of secretaries, since, even though volunteers might participate in the work of the organization, ultimately the professional worker was accountable for the provision of service. Urice spoke of lay control without mentioning boards. This manner of speaking, typical of many YMCA authors, was undoubtedly deliberate—the association cherished the notion of a democratic organization that would permit all members to participate in its policies. Councils and committees encouraged free discussion of association policy. But the prerogative of final decision regarding policy and finance rested with national and local association boards.

Lloyd L. McClow described the lines of authority within the YMCA, in his manual on volunteers. Using the image of a man with clasped hands to signify unity, he explained that the board of directors was the head controlling two arms—the committees and the secretarial staff.[18]

But the analogy of hands meekly obeying the head did not always hold. Some board members wistfully remembered the time when executives sat outside the boardroom door and were told afterward what had been decided. Docility was no longer characteristic of administrators. In large YMCA associations, one speaker noted at a meeting of the National Social Work Council in 1939, executives who attended board meetings "are very like businessmen and they seem to sit together quite on a par in matters of policy and finance."[19] Secretaries were giving too little attention to laymen and neglecting board members. Sherrard Ewing of Travelers Aid objected to the influence of Community Chests, which took from local laymen their one source of power—the responsibility for raising money.[20]

Elwood Street noted that on occasion executives, who expected all their proposals to be rubber-stamped, dominated their boards by offering their resignation whenever they were crossed.[21] Resistence was urged. A bulletin of the Boston Council of Social Agencies listed the qualities board members should have: willingness to work, intelligence, ability to think, an inquiring attitude, patience, courage, openmindedness, recognition of other's opinions, and pride in the traditions of the agency. No executive could ruffle a board member possessing these qualities, but where outside Boston could such virtue be found?

Addressing settlement board members at the annual NFS conference in 1937, Mrs. George Klein, experienced in the ways of boards through long service on boards and their committees, was critical of board behavior. She took as a case illustration the work of Detroit's NFS Board Member Division, an amalgamation of settlement boards in that city. Although board members had rallied to a call for city-wide cooperation during the early years of the depression, it was difficult to sustain their interest.[22] Lack of interest and commitment were frequently cited as the reasons why so many boards were "long, dry and narrow." Boredom bred formalism that expressed itself in an eagerness to cut debate on an issue by a resolution, any resolution.

More persistent still was the complaint that boards claimed to represent the agency constituents or clients without being truly representative. Problems of finance and the need for business leadership in rallying community support placed businessmen in a strong position on agency boards, and executives acquiesced to their dominance. Yet most agency officials spoke of boards as though these boards represented their communities, and hardly an article was written on the subject of boards or an address delivered without some reference to democracy.

The YMCA and the YWCA were aware of inconsistencies in faith and practice, for they in particular considered themselves "membership-participating agencies."[23] The YWCA was especially concerned with the need to represent working girls on boards and committees. Delegates to the National Industrial Assembly passed two resolutions in 1934: (1) that, where industrial girls were not included on boards and committees, an éffort should be made to include them; (2) that meetings of boards and committees be held in the evening so that industrial girls could attend. While most associations took note of the recommendations, no effective action resulted. Two years later a committee reported that "only a few associations are democratic in the election of board members—most Associations do not have a choice of ballot."[24] Where associations allowed more than one choice on the ballot, working girls were seldom nominated, since they were not on nominating committees. Often they were not even voting members of the YWCA. The industrial department of the association made no accusation that elections were rigged; it felt rather that local associations observed the letter of the law and ignored its spirit. In 1936 the industrial department mounted a campaign to encourage working girls to take an active part in association politics. It initiated discussions, produced morality plays on participation, and instructed working girls in parliamentary procedure and community organization. The industrial department realized that if working girls were to share in policy making they would have to take time to organize and to train themselves for responsibility.

Social workers who promoted social action sometimes blamed boards for hampering constructive programs in social welfare. Helen Hall, president of the National Federation of Settlements, complained that those elements in the community on whom social workers most depended were often opposed to preventive action and social planning.[25] She cited cases where agency boards in New York and elsewhere opposed the efforts of indigenous groups to organize. At a FWAA meeting in Minneapolis in 1931 one of the participants (a board member) remarked that some boards were even reluctant to allow secretaries to mention unemployment at board meetings. What was the use of a board, he asked, if it refused to discuss underlying causes that brought people to welfare agencies?[26]

Not all blame could be placed at the boardroom door. Agency executives sought boards that had financial, social, or political influence and, more often than not, they got the boards they desired. In the early depression, of thirty-four New York City settlement administrators responding to the question, "Does anyone from the neighborhood other than the head worker serve on the board?" Twenty-five answered, "No," and nine said, "Yes."[27] One settlement, which at one time had local young men and women making up the entire board, gradually replaced these, so that eventually no one from the neighborhood had a place on the governing board. The administrator of the settlement, explaining the change in board

106

membership, said that the house needed money and the local representatives were unable to assume financial obligations.

In 1930 Owen Pence made a survey of 560 YMCA local boards of directors. He gathered information on 9,459 board members ranging in age from 18 to 86 years, with a median of 47.6 years. Regarding the education of board members, 55.2 percent were college graduates; 13.5 percent had completed some graduate work beyond the fourth year in college. This educational distribution represented an average approximately two years beyond that of secretaries then in service. Although a few members had served on boards more than fifty years, the median tenure was five years. One in eight had served ten years or more. Annual service hours ranged from 20 to 150. Businessmen predominated as board members; only one in six could be considered a professional person.[28] The principal occupations and the percentages of YMCA board members so occupied in 1930 were: business and industrial occupations (61.2), professional occupations (20.9), clerical (5.1), unskilled labor (3.5), retired (2.7), skilled labor (1.7), agricultural (1.3), miscellaneous (3.6).

If the results of a 1935 study of FWAA boards were typical of other family societies throughout the decade, family agencies relied on professionals to serve as board members more than did the YMCA or, apparently, settlement houses. The total number of board members studied was 4,208 in 179 private agencies. Figures from the 1935 annual report of FWAA member agencies indicate the following composition of boards: professional (25.5), business people (27.8), housewives (11.1), public officials (1.5), retired (2.5), miscellaneous (1.9) no profession or business (4.4), not known (25.3).[29]

The constitution or by-laws of agencies generally determined the size of boards. Street, in his textbook on administration, advocated boards comprised of 15 to 30 members.[30] But boards were sometimes larger than that. The FWAA yearly report of 1935 showed 156 agencies with boards of 15 to 30 members, nine with boards of 35 to 50 members, and four with boards of more than 50 members.[31] Some provision for rotating membership was practically universal in FWAA. The constitutions of many other agencies provided for rotation in office by forbidding the immediate re-election of a board member after he served his term, but this rotation plan was not always followed.

The orientation and training of board members were generally informal, although the need for more extensive education was often expressed. At a symposium on settlement boards in the summer of 1934, participating board members asked for training in decision making concerning the choice of agency executives and staff, new board members, and officers of boards. They also requested education in settlement work. Some agencies provided formal training for their board members or sent their board members to institutes and conferences. The Connecticut State Conference of Social Work held a board members institute in 1931. The topics discussed included:[32]

1. What qualifications should a board member have?
2. What should a board member know and how should he inform himself?
3. What is the division of responsibility between the board member and the executive staff?

Placement bureaus, which played an important role in promoting volunteer activity during the depression, paid scant attention to the education of boards. Although one of their aims was the instruction of board members they were remiss in their duty. The St. Louis bureau was the only one that offered a course for the further education of board members. The course consisted of a series of ten one-hour lectures, twice a week for five weeks. The subject matter of the course covered the relationship between board and staff, the duties of the board, the board member's individual responsibility, principles of organization, the membership of a board, the functions of committees, and the relationship of the board to the community. Some placement bureaus—Chicago, Cleveland, and Milwaukee—held one-day institutes for board members. Beyond this, the bureaus offered little to board members apart from general orientation courses open to all volunteers.

Lacking regular training courses, board members fell back on informal means of acquiring social work knowledge—by conversations with other board members or conducted tours through the neighborhood, with a social worker as guide. In addition, some organizations prepared manuals for board members. The YMCA published *The Guide Book for Volunteers* principally for the use of board and committee members; FWAA had *A Handbook for Board Members and Volunteers*. Board members also attended the meetings of service volunteers to learn about agency programs. Many board members undertook a kind of in-service training by assuming extra responsibilities in visiting their community, serving on city-wide committees, doing clerical work and research.

Board membership alone never fulfilled the requirements of citizen participation. Thorough participation would have meant giving clients access to power through political and reform activity. Some social workers saw this clearly; others, darkly. Elements in social work's own past obscured the vision. The old COS movement had been oligarchical in its organization and procedures, and the family societies, which grew out of the movement, carried on the same traditions. When the Brooklyn Bureau of Charities, during the long cold winter of 1932–33, had its clients distribute food tickets and organize groups for "economic self-help," such as bartering and gardening, it was not really breaking new ground, although social workers proclaimed the project an innovation. Helping the poor help themselves had always been part of the COS credo. Self-help among the poor was achieved under the direction of board members and staff. However social workers and their committees might quarrel among themselves, most were confident of a combined power to do good. Since family societies had as their "fundamental task . . . an analytic approach to the problems of the individual family which . . . failed in its social adjustment," it followed that any endeavor to give members of the family further experience in group activities always remained secondary to the principal duty of the family agency.[33] Though heavy caseloads and increasing demands made family societies reassess their use of manpower, the resulting experimentation was kept within bounds. The rediscovery of the volunteer did not involve the discovery of the client as an indigenous leader. Clients might deliver food packages; they did not set policy. When trained workers were lacking, "intelligent well educated, socially minded volunteers" took their place, but even these worked "under trained leaders at properly selected tasks."[34]

Critics castigated the settlement movement for failing to live up to its professional belief in citizen participation at the neighborhood level. At a 1930 symposium on settlement faith and good works a speaker asked, "Is Democracy in America dead? If it is not, then why is it so dead in the settlements? Do we want to prepare young people for participation in a better political life than we now have? The settlement is an excellent training ground. But paternalism and maternalism are quite the rule."[35]

Dialogue sometimes took the place of political activism in the

109

settlements. A Chicago neighborhood house organized weekly discussions for the unemployed. The aim was a modest one: "to interpret the depression to the men who applied to the social worker for aid." The group screened its members and rigidly excluded communists.[36] The caution was a response to fear. Baden Street Settlement of Rochester, New York, echoed this anxiety when it stated in a policy report, "Grouping of the unemployed is not a particularly safe arrangement," and urged instead that the jobless associate with the employed.[37] But there was a greater danger in discouraging the participation of the unemployed in discussions on welfare problems —the jobless might become a menace to society. At any rate, that was the threat that Lea Taylor, a Chicago settlement worker, held over those who opposed such meetings. She warned that unemployed men and women, time hanging heavily on their hands, with no money to spend and feeling themselves outcasts from society, would soon become a danger to the same society unless they were allowed to express themselves and to take an active part in the life of their community.[38]

On occasion settlements went beyond discussion to agitation. Senator Robert Wagner, in his fight for better housing, had the support of settlement leaders such as Mary Simkhovitch and Helen Aldred.[39] The alliance meant more than the cooperation of high-minded people. The settlements were in a position to organize pavement democracy. The League of Mothers' Clubs of the New York settlements took to the streets. They gathered signatures for a petition to President Roosevelt. The first pages of the portfolio the League prepared ("as big as an unabridged dictionary") were devoted to photographs of windowless interior rooms, common hall toilets, and corridors that were firetraps. The tenement mothers carried their petition to the White House.[40] The tactics brought accusations of communism. Not only were settlement board members and the well-to-do suspicious, but slum dwellers themselves voiced concern for, as one of them remarked on seeing a settlement protest march, "only Communists want better houses."[41]

To keep social work activity in perspective, it must be remembered that social workers were by no means the only ones engaged in community organization. Numerous "workers alliance" groups, Townsend groups, and women's associations organized volunteers in the cause of local and national reform. The prominent women's associations in particular, though they were not precisely social wel-

110

fare organizations, agitated for labor legislation, child and maternal care, and social security. The National Consumers' League, for instance, in its defense of the Wagner Act with its sanction of collective bargaining, behaved as a pressure group on behalf of those too bewildered or scattered by exploitation to act for themselves.[42] The League of Women Voters encouraged the active participation of its members, all volunteers, in the political arena.[43] These associations and others like them understood the notion of grass-root democracy, and experienced the same frustrations as the settlement movement in making it a reality.

Summary

The role of the citizen in social planning and control remained ambiguous in New Deal philosophy. Whether the emphasis on citizen consultation through advisory boards and committees was promoted to further participation for its own sake is uncertain. If this was the intention, citizen participation was a failure. The National Youth Administration made more of an effort than most other federal agencies to involve the various sectors of the community—education, labor, business, agriculture, and the minority groups—in its decisions and actions; but youth, labor, and the minority groups were never properly represented. S. Burns Weston, who believed in decentralized administration, was trapped by his own code. The NYA advisory boards came up against the vested interests of state and local administrators. Although every state had its youth advisory board, a full 38 percent did not convene them during the year 1939–40, while eleven other state advisory boards met only once during that year. At the local level, public officials sometimes made up entire NYA advisory committees. If, however, the intention of NYA was not to achieve broad representation, as it professed, but rather to further the administration's programs, then the venture was more successful than the surveys on representation would indicate. There are some indications that political expediency, and not any theoretical espousal of volunteer participation, dictated the administration's policy of citizen consultation. NYA's recommendations in 1940 for "good selections of representation" were entirely pragmatic.[44] The New Deal administration apparently used advisory boards in much the same way as private family agencies used committees: to sound

111

out community opinion and to interpret its programs to the public. Where the ballot box was the principal criterion of democracy, community participation could remain secondary to the government's fundamental responsibility to provide for the general welfare of its citizens.

The public seemed satisfied with its right to vote. In fact, it was wary of handing over to unpaid citizens wide discretionary powers. Pierce Atwater might object that "academic concepts of freedom" permitted inferior forms of government to flourish, but elected officials could be held accountable for their actions in a way that unpaid persons could not. Lay governing boards of public welfare agencies dropped from favor in the 1930s, as social service moved further into the public and political domain. Advisory committees frequently graced public welfare agencies, but effective power belonged to the department head who was responsible to the elected official or group that appointed him. Where citizen boards did rule, they seldom had executive duties—the execution of policy belonged to the welfare bureaucracy.

Organized social work was New Deal in mind and heart. The congressional hearings on social welfare during the early part of the decade left congressmen and their constituents in no doubt as to where the profession stood. Also, the American Association of Social Workers and the American Public Welfare Association formally recommended a national program of social welfare. But the firm commitment to overhead planning made citizen participation so much more difficult, and social workers succeeded no better than other New Dealers in finding a solution to the problem. The glorification of boards, eulogies on the art of conference, and dissertations on integrative socialization could never hide the profession's discomfort with its own power. Uneasy heads pondered the meaning of power-with and power-over in the hope of finding a formula that would combine centralized planning with maximum lay participation. But the stakes were too high to ignore the one essential of planning and execution—expertise.

Efforts to broaden the base of power by seating community leaders on policy-making boards salved consciences without destroying oligarchies. Times were hard, and even the settlements, which professed belief in client participation and indigenous leadership, had to look for wealthy board members. Aside from financial considerations, other factors had to be taken into account—prestige, social

112

standing, and brute political influence. Organized social work was dedicated to a program of social reform, and it found what allies it could.

Some use was made of indigenous leadership in the settlements, some client participation in the family agencies, a concern for democracy in the group work agencies as exemplified by the effort to promote working girls in the YWCA hierarchy, but all this is not enough to dispel the impression that the social reform movement of the 1930s was mainly middle class. The potentiality of mass movements to become violent bred caution. Yet despite the fears of those who saw in unemployment the risk of upheaval or the hopes of those who perceived a force for social reformation, men roaming the streets seldom amounted to anything more organized than men roaming the streets.

CHAPTER 7

• • •

Summary

• • •

When the economy of the 1920s collapsed, the nation declared, as well it might, an emergency. Initial attempts to wish away the evil by ascribing it to the vicissitudes of growth were a shock reaction more than anything else and could not be sustained. The crisis demanded a solution. Efforts to peg down wages and prices and to stimulate credit seemed to promise the simplest and best remedy of all, economic expansion. Hoover's pledge to support public and private construction was not a hollow one, but his intention to keep the federal government "within its own province" hampered effective action. Hoover refused to make the Reconstruction Finance Corporation an instrument of massive government intervention, although he could claim that in lending money to the states for direct assistance and work relief he had honored his promise of federal aid. Basic to Hoover's philosophy and behind his reliance on presidential committees on employment was the belief that an all-out voluntary effort on the part of business, industry, labor, and the social welfare community offered the surest hope of recovery.

President Hoover's attitude was not unique; congressmen, business leaders, Red Cross officials, speakers at the National Conference of Social Work, and the public as a whole saw the need to mobilize all possible resources. The emergency, of course, required measures wholly pleasing to no one. The decade of normalcy had been a settled period in which people could go about their business. The onset of the depression brought disharmony in the sense that ordinary hierarchical principles and standard practices were held in doubt. In the field of organized social work this was so. The family agencies had to abandon tradition for a time, and concentrate on direct relief rather than on social therapy. In order to administer extensive relief programs, agencies called upon volunteers and occasionally had more volunteers than paid staff in their employment. Not only that. Distinctions in job function began to look slightly irrelevant. Feeding the hungry and clothing the naked were immediate necessities, and, given the provisions, the volunteer could do these as well as the professional. Some group work organizations, notably the settlements, objected to the new tasks that the public asked of them, but they too had to shoulder relief responsibilities. Volunteers, often untrained, took up positions in settlements when money to pay professional workers ran low. The Red Cross, which entered unemployment relief through the backdoor of disaster assistance, was not clear where its duty lay and could not define with any assurance the functions of its chapter members. The factors determining volunteer participation in services of relief and care were many—the manpower shortage, public opinion, political attitudes toward government assistance, professional ideas regarding the function of social work, and the job market itself. In the early days of the depression especially no one was quite sure how these elements related nor could people easily discern a pattern. As a consequence, the position of the volunteer in social service tended to be ambiguous.

The 1932 elections were a mandate for change in government policy. Measures such as the Agricultural Adjustment Act (1933), the key legislation of the National Recovery Act (1933) with provision for the alphabetic agencies, and the Social Security Act (1935) altered the nation's economic and welfare patterns. Though the statutes did not inaugurate social planning, they intensified it. New Deal programs, with their emphasis on proper administration and accountability, strengthened the welfare bureaucracies. State welfare departments used volunteers on boards and in direct service, but the principal value of volunteers, in the eyes of administrators, was the volunteers' potential to broaden the area of service and to lend public support to the new agencies. Social workers, expert in management and human relations, were the chief promoters of social welfare. Volunteers were aides.

Organized social work welcomed government intervention and not wholly for selfish reasons. At congressional hearings from 1930 onward social workers testified to the bankruptcy of private welfare and to the worsening plight of the unemployed. Social work associations followed the lead of National Conferences of social work in clamoring for government action that went far beyond coordination and supplementary assistance. When the Roosevelt administration passed extensive social legislation, there was within the profession some murmuring that planned security was not enough, that citizens should also participate in welfare policy and execution. In general, however, the profession was content to leave well-enough alone. The public was apathetic. Satisfied with its right to vote, it made no demand that citizen boards take over government agencies or programs. Government advisory boards and policy boards of private agencies provided some citizen involvement though without achieving the sort of grass-root democracy that community organizers would have liked. The settlements, the Ys, and other group work agencies continued to laud indigenous leadership, but their works did not reflect their faith in any outstanding way.

The division of labor according to expertise (which meant in practice giving volunteers routine tasks to perform) became increasingly prevalent as the depression wore on. There were many reasons for this. First of all, government intervention released the family agencies from the major responsibility for relief. Remedial casework could reassert itself, and the "proper function" of the family agency became once again apparent. The dominance of the professional in casework was traditional. Even during the early emergency, there were agencies—the child welfare agencies, for instance—that held the line and did not allow volunteers to take over professional duties. Supervision and training, while improving skill, served also to remind the volunteer that a little learning, though not dangerous, fell short of mastery.

The area where volunteers were most dominant throughout the depression was group work. Volunteers, with varying degrees of training, carried the chief responsibility for group leadership. The professional seldom directed groups; his tasks were mainly administrative and supervisory. Group work was in the process of development, but it did not, could not, claim a body of knowledge uniquely its own that was comparable to casework's skill in diagnosis and treatment. The ultimate criterion of professional status in every branch of social work was specialization, and in this group work was lacking. Although undoubtedly recreation, education, and generic social work provided a base of knowledge and skill, group work itself was still an uncertain science. Research pertinent to group work theory and practice revealed the first blades of specialization, but the harvest was not yet.

Samuel Mencher, writing on voluntarism in general, has stated,

"The role of voluntary activity has been intimately connected with two major developments in the twentieth century: the rise of governmental responsibility for social welfare and the growth of social work as a profession."[1] What Mencher has written of voluntary activity in social welfare applies with equal validity to the use of volunteers in the 1930s. The government's role, which expanded under the New Deal, threatened a tradition of voluntarism. The advocates of social planning were seldom quite logical when discussing citizen participation. Taking a leaf from their critics, they espoused participation as though no dilemma existed. But universal participation in social welfare was more easily preached than practiced. The growing complexity of social service demanded specialized personnel who were at home in dealing with problems of unemployment, relief, child welfare, psychosocial rehabilitation, and family security. A bureaucracy, based on expertise, directed social welfare, and no alternative appeared feasible. While the magnitude of the social task made volunteer participation essential, volunteers were by and large ancillary to professionals during the depression. Nonetheless, they shared with social workers one goal, the common good. In the end it was this shared concern for the general welfare that kept the New Deal as close as the times permitted to the nation's democratic traditions.

117

For the sake of simplicity, we have generally abbreviated the titles of manuscript collections as well as of associations whose material we have used. Reference to particular archives and agencies simply means that the cited documents, either in their original form or on microfilm, may be found there.

In the notes we have used the following abbreviations:

AAMSW Papers: American Association of Medical Social Workers (University of Minnesota Social Welfare History Archives)

AJLA Papers: Association of Junior Leagues of America (University of Minnesota Social Welfare History Archives)

Baden Street Settlement Papers: Baden Street Settlement (University of Minnesota Social Welfare History Archives)

Big Brothers Papers: Big Brothers of America (University of Minnesota Social Welfare History Archives)

Big Sisters Papers: Big Sisters, Inc. (University of Minnesota Social Welfare History Archives)

CWLA Papers: Child Welfare League of America (University of Minnesota Social Welfare History Archives)

FERA Papers: Federal Emergency Relief Administration (National Archives)

FSAA Papers: (Family Service Association of America, New York)

NCCC Proceedings: National Conference on Charities and Correction

NCL Papers: National Consumers' League (Library of Congress)

NCSW Proceedings: National Conference of Social Work

NFS Papers: National Federation of Settlements (University of Minnesota Social Welfare History Archives)

NLWV Papers: National League of Women Voters (Schlesinger Library, Radcliffe College)

NSWA Papers: National Social Welfare Assembly (University of Minnesota Social Welfare History Archives)

NYA Papers: National Youth Administration (National Archives)

PRCST Papers: President's Research Committee on Social Trends (Library of Congress)

Survey Associates Papers: Survey Associates (University of Minnesota Social Welfare History Archives)

TAAA Papers: Travelers Aid Association of America (University of Minnesota Social Welfare History Archives)

UCFCA Papers: United Community Funds and Councils of America (University of Minnesota Social Welfare Archives)

UNH Papers: United Neighborhood Houses of New York (University of Minnesota Social Welfare History Archives)

WPA Papers: Works Projects Administration (National Archives)

YMCA Papers: Young Men's Christian Association (YMCA Historical Library, New York)

YWCA Papers: Young Women's Christian Association (YWCA Library, New York)

INTRODUCTION

1. See Frank Reisman and Arthur Pearl, *New Careers for the Poor* (Glencoe, Ill.: Free Press, 1965).

2. Classifying the YMCA and the YWCA as general character-building organizations rather than as Protestant religious associations was not unusual in the 1930s. See, for instance, M. M. Chambers, *Youth-Serving Organizations* (Washington, D.C.: American Council on Education, 1937), pp. 37–39.

3. Harold Wilensky and Charles N. Lebeaux, *Industrial Society and Social Welfare* (New York: Russell Sage Foundation, 1958), p. 17.

CHAPTER 1

1. A. W. Guttridge, "The Volunteer Worker," NCCC *Proceedings* (1903), p. 307.

2. Frederick Almy in a discussion, NCCC *Proceedings* (1903), p. 564.

3. Mary Richmond, NCCC *Proceedings.* (1903), p. 564.

4. Daniel Thurz, *Volunteer Group Advisors in a National Social Group Work Agency* (Washington, D.C.: Catholic University of America Press, 1960), p. 49.

5. Annual Report for 1901, cited in *Baden Street Settlement* (Rochester: Verway Printing Co., 1929), p. 5.

6. A. W. Guttridge, "Needy Families: Their Homes and Neighborhoods: Report of the Committee," NCCC *Proceedings* (1907), p. 301.

7. Luther Gulick quoted in C. Howard Hopkins, *History of the*

YMCA in North America (New York: Association Press, 1951), p. 481.

8. Helen F. Barnes, *The Volunteer Worker* (New York: YWCA, 1907), p. 4.

9. Mary Richmond, "Friendly Visitors," NCCC *Proceedings* (1907), p. 315.

10. Annual Report (1914), Big Sisters Papers.

11. Mary C. Goodwillie, "Efficiency in the Use of Volunteers," NCCC *Proceedings* (1915), p. 86.

12. *Report of the Commission on Training of Volunteer Workers of the Young Women's Christian Association of America,* YWCA Conference Report (Apr. 1913), YWCA Papers, Film File 115–4.

13. Wanda Greineisen, "Serving and Training Club Leaders," address before NFS Conference (June 1917), NFS Papers.

14. Constance McL. Green, "The History of the American National Red Cross," vol. 21, "The Origins and Developments of the Home Service Corps, 1917–47" (Washington, D.C.: American National Red Cross, 1950), pp. 5–6 (mimeographed).

15. Karl de Schweinitz, "Avocational Guidance," NCSW *Proceedings* (1917), p. 118.

16. Frank J. Bruno, *Trends in Social Work, 1874–1956* (New York: Columbia University Press, 1957), p. 39.

17. Robert H. Bremner, *From the Depths* (New York: New York University Press, 1956), p. 54.

18. Richard Hofstadter, *The Age of Reform* (New York: Vintage Books, 1955), pp. 148–64.

19. Roy Lubove, *The Professional Altruist* (Cambridge: Harvard University Press, 1965), p. 164.

20. Gertrude Vaile in a discussion on the topic, "Family Treatment in War Time Community Programs," NCSW *Proceedings* (1918), p. 368.

21. Green, "The History of the American National Red Cross," 21:15.

22. Foster Rhea Dulles, *The American Red Cross* (New York: Harper, 1950), p. 236.

23. Constance McL. Green and Harold R. Hutcheson, "The History of the American National Red Cross," (Washington, D.C.: American National Red Cross, 1950), 8:26.

24. Lea D. Taylor, Winifred Salisbury, and Harriet E. Vittum, *The Administration and Activities of Chicago Settlements* (Boston: National Federation of Settlements, 1921).

25. Albert J. Kennedy, Kathryn Farra, et al., *Social Settlements in New York City* (New York: Columbia University Press, 1935), pp. 32–33.

26. Owen E. Pence, *The YMCA and Social Need* (New York: Associated Press, 1939), p. 180.

27. *Report on a Survey of the International Committee of YMCA's of North America* (The Jones Report, New York, 1923), p. 3.

28. Executive Committee Minutes (13–14 Mar. 1924), CWLA Papers, Microfilm 2, Reel 1.

29. *Family Life in America Today,* report prepared for FWAA Conference (Oct. 1927), FSAA Papers.

30. Sidney Fine, *Laissez-faire and the General Welfare State; A Study of Conflict in American Thought, 1865–1901* (Ann Arbor: University of Michigan Press, 1956).

CHAPTER 2

1. Note to Arthur Kellogg in the handwriting of Gertrude Springer, an associate editor. Survey Associates Papers, Folder 852.

2. Clare M. Tousley, "Volunteer—1932 Model," *Survey* 67:10 (15 Dec. 1932), p. 34.

3. Wendell F. Johnson, "How Case Working Agencies Have Met Unemployment," NCSW *Proceedings* (1931), p. 190.

4. Ibid., p. 195.

5. Caroline Bedford, "The Effect of an Employment Situation in Family Societies," NCSW *Proceedings* (1931), p. 203.

6. *Social Work Yearbook* (1931), p. 546.

7. William Hodson, "The Effect of the Depression on Professional Standards," NCSW *Proceedings* (1932) p. 535.

8. R. C. Davison, "England's Experience with Unemployment Insurance and the Dole," NCSW *Proceedings* (1932), p. 88.

9. Here we have relied heavily on Irving Bernstein, *The Lean Years* (Baltimore: Penguin Books, 1966), pp. 302–10. Bernstein's Chap. 8, "The Breakdown of Local Resources," contains a succinct but perceptive account of the failure and frustration of PECE.

10. Ellery F. Reed, "Efforts of Social Workers towards Social Reorganization," *Social Forces* 14 (1935), pp. 87–93.

11. Ibid.

12. Robert E. Bondy, "The Volunteer in the Rural Community," NCSW *Proceedings* (1933), p. 437.

13. Hertha Kraus, "Lay Participation in Social Work as It Affects the Public Agency," NCSW *Proceedings* (1934), p. 223.

14. Mary van Kleeck, "Our Illusions Regarding Government," NCSW *Proceedings* (1934), p. 481.

15. Eduard C. Lindeman, "Basic Unities in Social Work," NCSW *Proceedings* (1934), p. 515.

16. Pierce Atwater, "The County as a Unit for Co-ordinate Planning and Service in Public and Private Social Work (Point of View of Private Agencies)," NCSW *Proceedings* (1937), p. 377.

17. Wilmer Shields, "The Importance of the Layman in Community Organization," NCSW *Proceedings* (1938), pp. 423–24.

18. Ruth Hyde Harvie, "Board Member Soul Searching," *Survey* 74:3 (Mar. 1938), p. 75.

19. Clarence King, "Social Agency Boards and How to Serve on Them," *Survey* 73:11 (Nov. 1937), pp. 342–44; 73:12 (Dec. 1937), pp. 378–79; 74:1 (Jan. 1938), pp. 12–13; 74:2 (Feb. 1938), pp. 41–42.

20. Ralph G. Hurlin and Anne E. Geddes, "Public and Private Unemployment Relief," NCSW *Proceedings* (1931), pp. 435–36. See also U.S. Bureau of the Census, *Relief Expenditures by Governmental and Private Organizations* (Washington, D.C.: Government Printing Office, 1932), p. 6.

21. Thurz, *Volunteer Group Advisors,* p. 81.

22. Roy Sorenson, "Group Work and Group Work Agencies in Recent Community Studies," NCSW *Proceedings* (1937), p. 299.

23. Arthur L. Swift, Jr., "The Essentials of Training for Group Leadership," NCSW *Proceedings* (1935), p. 365.

24. Arthur L. Swift, Jr., "Training Aspects of Group Work," paper read at the Group Work Section, New York State Conference of Social Work, 1935, NFS Papers, Folder 75.

CHAPTER 3

1. Mollie Ray Carrol, "Maintaining Morale in a Crisis," mimeographed report on University of Chicago Settlement, 1931–32 (14 June 1932), NFS Papers, Folder 539.

2. Annual report (Oct. 1930), Baden Street Settlement Papers, Folder 39.

3. "Ways in which Settlements Have Adjusted Their Work to Reduced Income," Detroit (8 June 1933), NFS Papers, Folder 79. See John M. Herrick, "A Holy Discontent: The History of the New York

City Social Settlements in the Inter-War Era, 1919–1941," Unpublished Ph.D. Dissertation (Minneapolis: University of Minnesota, 1970).

4. Annual Report of the Executive Director (May 1932), CWLA Papers, Film 2, Reel 1.

5. Ibid.

6. CWLA *Special News Letter* 5 (15 May 1933), CWLA Papers.

7. CWLA *Special News Letter* 1 (17 Mar. 1933), CWLA Papers.

8. Meta Gruner, "Volunteers in a Children's Agency," CWLA *Bulletin* (May 1933), p. 2, CWLA Papers.

9. Excerpt from a speech by Emma C. Puschner, "The Volunteer in Child Welfare," delivered at a "Century of Progress" Child Welfare Meeting in Chicago (27 June 1933), CWLA *Special News Letter* 8 (17 July 1933), p. 4, CWLA Papers.

10. Cooperation was especially important in small rural municipalities that lacked adequate public welfare services. See Edmund de S. Brunner and J. H. Kolb, *Rural Social Trends* (New York: McGraw-Hill, 1933), pp. 271–73; PRCST Papers, Folders entitled, "Emmett, Idaho," "Arcadia, Wisconsin," "Medford, Wisconsin," and "Litchfield, Minnesota."

11. Mimeographed draft of "The Use of Volunteers in Children's Agencies and Institutions," (New York: Child Welfare League of America, 1937), p. 9, CWLA Papers.

12. Ibid., pp. 4–8.

13. Dulles, *The American Red Cross,* p. 286.

14. Ibid., p. 288.

15. The Civil Works Administration, which at its peak in 1934 employed over four million workers, was operated exclusively by the federal government. The cost of CWA (expenditures for a six-month period reached $863,965,000) persuaded Congress to liquidate the program shortly after its inception and to substitute a more efficient Works Progress Administration. WPA, also a work relief project, differed from CWA in that it took all its employees from relief rolls, whereas CWA had been willing to hire people in general need of work; moreover, WPA paid a "security wage" without reference to family size and dependents. The Civilian Conservation Corps (1933) and the National Youth Administration (1935) were essentially training and work programs for unemployed youth. Each of the federal programs was a departure from total reliance upon local, state, and private institutions to solve the problem of unemployment and in-

security. For a synoptic description of the New Deal social welfare programs, see Walter A. Friedlander, *Introduction to Social Welfare,* 2nd ed. (Englewood Cliffs, N.J.: Prentice-Hall, 1961), pp. 117–35.

16. Doris Carothers, *Chronology of the Federal Emergency Relief Administration* (Washington, D.C.: Government Printing Office, 1937), p. 19.

17. "Introduction to Casework and Administration of Relief" (Washington, D.C.: American Red Cross, 1933), p. 1 (mimeographed).

18. Dulles, *The American Red Cross,* p. 2.

19. "Introduction to Casework," p. 19.

20. Mary F. Bogue, "The Effect upon Standards of Our Present Economic Depression and What We Must Do about It," address before the New York State Conference of Social Work (11 Nov. 1931), FSAA Papers.

21. Typewritten report of Self-Study Committee on Volunteers, Philadelphia Family Society, 1931, FSAA Papers.

22. Ibid., p. 5.

23. Ibid., p. 7.

24. Supplement to FWAA *News Letter* 7:1 (Mar. 1932), p. 1, FSAA Papers.

25. Ibid, p. 6.

26. Helen I. Clarke, "The Future of the Emergency Worker," *The Compass* 14:2 (Oct. 1932), p. 3.

27. Office memorandum (20 Jan. 1932), Jewish Social Service Bureau, Cleveland, FSAA Papers.

28. Arthur M. Schlesinger, Jr., *The Crisis of the Old Order* (Boston: Houghton Mifflin Co., 1957), p. 169.

29. Hurlin and Geddes, NCSW *Proceedings* (1931), pp. 435–36.

30. Margaret E. Rich, *A Belief in People* (New York: Family Service Association of America, 1956), p. 119.

31. *A Survey of the Social Agencies of Plainfield, New Jersey,* (New York: Community Chest and Council, 1936), p. 3, UNH Papers.

32. *FWAA News Letter* 7:7 (Nov. 1932), p. 29, FSAA Papers.

33. Quoted by Alice F. Liveright, "Possibilities of Volunteer Service in Public Agencies," NCSW *Proceedings* (1933), p. 443.

34. Margaret E. Rich, "Orientation of Emergency Unemployment Workers," a mimeographed outline of a study course (Sept. 1933), FSAA Papers.

CHAPTER 4

1. Ruth M. Dodd, *Volunteer Values* (New York: Family Welfare Association of America, 1934), p. 7

2. Miriam Van Waters, "The New Morality and the Social Worker," NCSW *Proceedings* (1929), p. 70.

3. Ibid., p. 65.

4. Ibid., p. 70.

5. Ethel Van Benthuyen, "The Volunteer Holds a Looking Glass," reprint from *The Family* (June 1933), p. 1, FSAA Papers.

6. See John C. Kidneigh, "The Concept of Development Which Underlies the Social Work Helping Process," in Dale B. Harris (ed.), *The Concept of Development* (Minneapolis: University of Minnesota Press, 1957), pp. 249–51. Kidneigh shows how the establishment of schools of social work within a university framework marked the end of that form of social work education that approximated apprenticeship training, and the beginning of a professional preparation based upon scientific knowledge.

7. *Social Work Year Book* (1935), p. 479.

8. Dorothy de la Pole, "Travelers Aid Field, 1922–1937," undated typescript (c. 1938), TAAA Papers, Microfilm 8, Reel 1. It should be noted, however, that De la Pole limited her attention to communities with populations of 2,500 and over.

9. Ibid.

10. Louise C. Odencrantz, *The Social Worker in Family, Medical and Psychiatric Social Work* (New York: Harper, 1929); Margaretta Williamson, *The Social Worker in Group Work* (New York: Harper, 1929); Margaretta Williamson, *The Social Worker in Child Care and Protection* (New York: Harper, 1931); Margaretta Williamson, *The Social Worker in the Prevention and Treatment of Delinquency* (New York: Columbia University Press, 1935); John A. Fitch, *Vocational Guidance in Action* (New York: Columbia University Press, 1935).

11. Williamson, *The Social Worker in the Prevention and Treatment of Delinquency*, p. x.

12. C. C. Carstens, "Some Conclusions Based on a Series of Studies by the Child Welfare League of America," NCSW *Proceedings* (1929), p. 116.

13. Kenneth H. Rogers, "A Study of the Big Brother and Big Sister Organizations of the United States and Canada on the Basis of a Survey of Local Organizations," mimeographed study by the Na-

tional Planning and Study Committee (Dec. 1940), pp. 23–24, Big Brothers Papers.

14. Ibid., p. 24.

15. See Richard C. Cabot, *Social Service and the Art of Healing* (New York: Moffat Yard, 1917), p. 178.

16. Helen B. Hooker to Marion Russell (22 Apr. 1942). AAMSW Papers, Folder entitled "Lay Participation Committee, 1935–1942,"

17. Report of Advisory Committee on Volunteers, Welfare Council of New York (Mar. 1940), AAMSW Papers.

18. Mimeographed job description manual of the Volunteer Bureau of Chicago's Council of Social Agencies (c. 1940), p. 8, AAMSW Papers.

19. Odencrantz, *The Social Worker in Family, Medical and Psychiatric Social Work*, p. 14.

20. *Social Work Year Book* (1935), p. 145.

21. Dodd, *Volunteer Values*, p. 10.

22. Mary Willcox Glenn, "Present Trends in the Family Welfare Field," reprint from *Junior League Magazine* (Mar. 1933), FSAA Papers.

23. Mrs. John Galbraith Pratt, "Lay Participation in Social Work: New Opportunities for the Volunteer," NCSW *Proceedings* (1934), pp. 217–22. The *Proceedings* contain only part of the address. The complete text may be found in *Junior League Magazine* (Oct. 1934), pp. 43–45, AJLA Papers.

24. Virginia Howlett, "Lay Participation in Social Work—From the Point of View of the Private Agency," reprint from *Junior League Magazine* (Oct. 1934), pp. 45–48, AJLA Papers.

25. Ibid., p. 45.

26. "A Manual for Volunteers," FWAA *News Letter* (Mar. 1936), p. 3, FSAA Papers.

27. A loose-leaf manual for volunteers prepared by the Family Welfare Society, Providence, R.I. (1935), FSAA Papers.

28. Evelyn P. Johnson to Margaret Wead (24 Apr. 1941), FSAA Papers.

29. "Service Analysis," mimeographed report by the Family Welfare Society of Rochester, New York (8 Sept. 1934), FSAA Papers.

30. *Volunteers for Family Service* (New York: Family Welfare Association of America, 1942), pp. 55–56.

31. Mimeographed Preliminary Report of the Committee on

Volunteers, Social Case Work Council of National Agencies (27 May 1941), FSAA Papers.

32. Summary report attached to the letter of Evelyn P. Johnson to Margaret Wead (24 Apr. 1941), FSAA Papers. For the sake of tidiness, we have converted all fractions of hours to their nearest whole numbers.

33. FWAA round-table discussion, Philadelphia (22 Mar.–3 Apr. 1936), FSAA Papers.

34. Dodd, *Volunteer Values,* p. 14.

35. Mimeographed suggestions for a central volunteer bureau by the Community Chests and Councils, New York (30 Dec. 1933), p. 1, FSAA Papers.

36. Florence L. Newbold, "A Community-Wide Volunteer Placement Bureau," NCSW *Proceedings* (1935), p. 468; and a Junior League list of volunteer bureaus in the U.S. (8 Aug. 1941), UCFCA Papers. The figures offered by Newbold and the Junior League may be no more than approximate.

37. Mrs. Thomas L. Tolan, "Analysis of Reports in a Survey of Volunteer Bureaus in the United States," report of the National Committee on Volunteers in Social Work (1935), p. 5.

38. Mrs. Thomas L. Tolan, "A Study of Volunteer Bureaus in the United States," report of the National Committee on Volunteers in Social Work (Apr. 1937), pp. 16–17.

39. Tolan, "Analysis of Report in a Survey of Volunteer Bureaus," p. 18.

40. *Volunteers for Family Service,* p. 23.

41. Mimeographed suggestions for an orientation course in social welfare by the Community Chests and Councils, New York (30 Dec. 1933), p. 2. FSAA Papers.

42. Pratt, NCSW *Proceedings,* (1934), p. 218.

CHAPTER 5

1. For a brief discussion on the political basis of voluntary associations, see Daniel Thurz, "Voluntarism: A Distinguishing Characteristic of America" in Nathan E. Cohen (ed.), *The Citizen Volunteer* (New York: Harper, 1960), pp. 22–23.

2. John Dewey, *Democracy and Education* (New York: Macmillan, 1961), p. iii.

3. Ibid., p. 99.

4. *Social Work Year Book* (1933), p. 482.

5. Ibid.

6. See Henry C. Metcalf and L. Urwick (eds.), *Dynamic Administration: The Collected Papers of Mary Parker Follett* (New York: Harper, 1942); also, Eduard C. Lindeman, "Mary Parker Follett," *Survey Graphic* 23:2 (Feb. 1934), p. 86.

7. Clara A. Kaiser (ed.), *Objectives of Group Work* (New York: Association Press, 1936), p. 20.

8. Charles E. Hendry in R. E. G. Davis, *A Primer of Guidance Through Group Work* (New York: Association Press, 1940), p. 5.

9. Eduard C. Lindeman, "The Roots of Democratic Culture," in *Group Work 1939* (New York: American Association for the Study of Group Work, 1939), p. 7.

10. Lindeman, "Youth and Leisure," *Annals of the American Academy of Political and Social Science* 194 (1937), p. 63.

11. *Social Work Year Book* (1933), p. 196.

12. Frank J. Bruno, *Trends in Social Work, 1874–1956* (New York: Columbia University Press, 1957), pp. 272–73.

13. E. S. Tachau, radio talk, WHAS, New York (1 Nov. 1932), NFS Papers; according to a note on the typescript, Mrs. Ralph E. Hill, a former resident of New York's Neighborhood House, wrote the address.

14. Clarke A. Chambers, *Seedtime of Reform* (Minneapolis: University of Minnesota Press, 1963), p. 146. *Seedtime's* Chap. 6—"The Settlement's Drive for Social Action"—contains a description, and an excellent discussion, of the settlement's role in reform during the decade of normalcy and reaction that followed World War I. But Chambers also points out (and settlement records support the statement) that the service aspects of settlement work took precedence over the commitment to social action in the postwar years. See Herrick, "A Holy Discontent: The History of the New York City Social Settlements, 1919–1941."

15. *Social Work Year Book* (1933), p. 483.

16. Annual report (31 Mar. 1932), p. 6, Baden Street Settlement Papers, Folder 37.

17. Typewritten draft of annual report (1 Apr. 1933), Baden Street Settlement Papers, Folder 37. Mrs. Grace Morris, a social worker in Baden Street's day nursery, prepared this part of the draft. The offending passage was penciled "omit."

18. Report (Nov. 1932), Baden Street Settlement Papers, Folder 37.

19. Helen Hart, "The Changing Function of the Settlement under Changing Conditions," NCSW *Proceedings* (1931), pp. 294–95.

20. *Social Work Year Book* (1933), p. 480–87.

21. Statistical Record (Apr. 1934), Baden Street Settlement Papers, Folder 59.

22. Henry M. Busch, "Rebuilding the Group Club," address before NFS Conference, Philadelphia (15 May 1932), NFS Papers, Folder 78.

23. *Social Work Year Book* (1935), p. 472.

24. Kennedy and Farra, *Social Settlements in New York City,* p. 50.

25. Statistical Records, Baden Street Settlement Papers, Box 5. As a basis for computation, we have taken those volunteers who regularly attended the settlements from April of one year to the following March.

26. *Social Work Year Book* (1933), p. 480.

27. Grace L. Coyle, *Group Work with American Youth* (New York: Harper, 1948), p. 12.

28. Williamson, *The Social Worker in Group Work,* p. 23.

29. Sorenson, NCSW *Proceedings* (1937), p. 299.

30. *Movement Trends,* Bureau of Records, Studies and Trends, Oct. 1936, p. 8, YMCA Papers.

31. L. L. McClow, "Volunteers for Class, Club and Committee" (Chicago, 1938), p. 14, mimeographed copy among YMCA Papers.

32. Chambers, *Youth-Serving Organizations,* pp. 27, 31.

33. See Williamson, *The Social Worker in Group Work,* pp. 7–19.

34. *Social Work Year Book* (1935), p. 459; see also Grace L. Coyle in *Social Work Year Book* (1937), pp. 461–64, for a discussion on the relationship between group work and recreation.

35. Allen T. Burns to Howard Braucher (19 Feb. 1936), NFS Papers, Folder 173; Louise F. Bache to Howard Braucher (7 Oct. 1935), Ibid.

36. David H. Holbrook to R. K. Atkinson (30 June 1933), Ibid.

37. LeRoy E. Bowman, "Application of Progressive Education Principles to Group Work," NCSW *Proceedings* (1931), pp. 315–22.

38. Wilbur I. Newstetter, *Wawokiye Camp: A Research Project in Group Work* (Cleveland: Western Reserve University, 1930), p. 43.

39. Helen Morton (ed.), *Clubs in Action: The Small Group Club* (Boston: Federation of Neighborhood Houses, 1934), pp. 5–8.

40. Elise Hatt Campbell, *Gauging Group Work: An Evaluation of a Settlement Boys' Work Program* (Detroit: National Youth Administration, 1938).

41. Harry D. Edgren, "Group Work in Health and Physical Education," in Charles E. Hendry (ed.), *A Decade of Group Work* (New York: Association Press, 1948), pp. 27–28.

42. W. I. Newstetter, "What Is Social Group Work?" NCSW *Proceedings* (1935), p. 291.

43. Harleigh B. Trecker (ed.), *Group Work Foundations and Frontiers* (New York: Whiteside, 1955), p. 3.

44. *Social Work Year Book* (1939), p. 413.

45. Charles E. Hendry, *The Group* (1939), quoted in Hendry, *A Decade of Group Work*, p. 153.

46. Classification of works (1935), FERA Papers, "New Subject" File No. 374; notes on women's work, FERA Papers, No. 375.

47. WPA Papers, Central Files (1935–44), Record Group 69, File 216.

48. Round-table discussion, "WPA Recreation Workers in Settlements," Philadelphia (May 1938), NFS Papers, Folder 599, p. 2.

49. Ibid.

50. Jeanette Dutchess, *The Program Volunteer in the YWCA* (New York: Woman's Press, 1937), pp. 7–10, YWCA Papers.

51. *YMCA Year Book* (1936), p. 34.

52. L. L. McClow, "Lay Leadership Commission," *Journal of Physical Education* 31:2 (Nov.–Dec. 1933), pp. 19–35; L. L. McClow, "Lay Leadership Appraisal," *Journal of Physical Education* 31:5 (May-June 1934), pp. 71–72, 80.

53. McClow, *Journal of Physical Education* 31:2 (Nov.–Dec. 1933), p. 19.

54. McClow, "Volunteers for Class, Club and Committee," p. 97.

55. McClow, "Lay Leadership," p. 59.

56. *YMCA Year Book* (1932), p. 29.

57. Sample Club Report (c. 1930), NFS Papers, Folder 75.

58. Model Airplane Records, NFS Papers, Folder 75.

59. Ibid.

60. Busch, "Rebuilding the Group Club," p. 6, NFS Papers, Folder 78.

61. Bertha C. Reynolds in her Foreword to Williamson, *Supervision of Volunteer Club Leaders*, p. 5.

62. Busch, "Rebuilding the Group Club," p. 7, NFS Papers, Folder 78.

63. Ray O. Wyland, *Principles of Scoutmastership* (New York: Boy Scouts of America, 1936), pp. 252–56.

64. McClow, "Lay Leadership," p. 11.

65. Swift, "Training Aspects of Group Work," NFS Papers, Folder 75.

66. McClow, "Volunteers for Class, Club and Committee," p. 61.

67. Hendry, NCSW *Proceedings* (1940), p. 547.

68. *Social Work Year Book* (1933), p. 547.

69. Albert Kennedy to Fred S. Hall (3 Sept. 1932), NFS Papers, Folder 546.

70. *Group Work 1939*, p. 58.

CHAPTER 6

1. Herbert Hoover, *The Challenge to Liberty* (New York: Charles Scribner's Sons, 1934), p. 17.

2. Van Kleeck, NCSW *Proceedings* (1934), pp. 473–86; Lindeman, ibid., pp. 504–17. Both speakers were recipients of the Pugsley Award that year for ". . . papers adjudged to have made the most important contribution to the subject matter of social work."

3. Arthur Dunham, "Public Relief—Mastery or Drift," *Survey* 70:12 (Dec. 1934), p. 381.

4. Pierce Atwater, "Powers and Functions of Lay Boards in Relation to Public Administration," NCSW *Proceedings* (1938), p. 522.

5. Helen E. Martz, *Citizen Participation in Government: A Study of County Welfare Boards* (Washington, D.C.: Public Affairs Press, 1948), p. 55–57.

6. Ibid.

7. Atwater, NCSW *Proceedings* (1938), pp. 518–27; Dunham, *Survey* 70:12 (Dec. 1934), p. 381.

8. *State and Local Welfare Organization in the State of New York*, report of the Governor's Commission on Unemployment Relief (28 Dec. 1935), pp. 59–61.

9. Marietta Stevenson, *Public Welfare Administration* (New York: Macmillan, 1938), p. 153.

10. Proceedings of a meeting of the National Advisory Committee of NYA (28–29 Aug. 1936), NYA Papers, Box 607.

11. Betty Lindley and Earnest K. Lindley, *A New Deal for Youth* (New York: Viking Press, 1938), p. 15.

12. Burns Weston to John Binns (7 Dec. 1940), NYA Papers, General Correspondence and Report File of the Director, 1935–42.

13. Mimeographed report of NYA Survey (Oct. 1940), NYA Papers, Box 608, pp. 2, 4.

14. Report of NYA Survey (Oct. 1940), p. 1, NYA Papers, Box 608. The exact yearly total member figures cannot be obtained by adding the respective categories. Apparently complete statistical accuracy was not important in the study.

15. Ibid., p. 7.

16. Margaret Rich, "Qualifications for Board Members," report of FWAA Survey (1937), FSAA Papers.

17. Jay A. Urice, "The Future of the Profession in Terms of the Lay-Professional Relationship," p. 2, located with minutes and papers for 1932–33, YMCA Papers.

18. McClow, "Volunteers for Class, Club and Committee," p. 121.

19. Minutes of National Social Work Council meeting, New York (18 Jan. 1929), NSWA Papers, Folder 39.

20. Minutes of National Social Work Council meeting, New York (18 Jan. 1929), NSWA Papers, Folder 39.

21. Elwood Street, *Social Work Administration* (New York: Harper, 1931), p. 7.

22. Mrs. George H. Klein, "Board Members' Cooperation in the Work of City and National Federation," address before NFS Conference (20 May 1937), p. 2, NFS Papers, Folder 83.

23. Lucille Lippitt, *The Guide Book for Volunteers* (New York: Woman's Press, 1932), p. 5.

24. Report to YWCA National Industrial Assembly (15 June 1936), YWCA Papers, Film file 115–4.

25. Helen Hall, "Social Work and Social Action," address before NFS Conference (23 May 1937), p. 1, NFS Papers, Folder 83.

26. Summary report of FWAA meeting, Minneapolis (June 1931), FSAA Papers.

27. Kennedy and Farra, *Social Settlements in New York City*, p. 488.

28. Pence, *The YMCA and Social Need*, p. 182.

29. Mimeographed statistical report (March 1936), FWAA Department of Studies and Information, FSAA Papers.

30. Street, *Social Work Administration*, p. 19.

31. Rich, "Qualifications of a Board Member," report of FWAA Survey (1937), FSAA Papers.

32. Dodd, *Volunteer Values,* p. 40.

33. Elizabeth Dutcher, "When Clients Participate," *Survey* 52:2 (Feb. 1934), p. 43.

34. Bogue, "The Effect Upon Standards of Our Present Economic Depression," FSAA Papers.

35. Algernon Black in "Settlement Faith and Practice: A Symposium by Headworkers Who Have Taken Office since 1915," *Neighborhood* 3:3 (Sept. 1930), p. 104; see also Walter Merritt and Isabel Merritt, "Democracy in the Settlements," *Neighborhood* 4:3 (Sept. 1931), pp. 157–71.

36. Carrol, "Maintaining Morale in a Crisis," pp. 4–5, NFS Papers, Folder 539.

37. Typewritten report (Oct. 1931) attached to the annual reports, 1926–35, Baden Street Settlement Papers.

38. Lea Taylor, quoted in clipping from *Knoxville Journal* (3 June 1936), UNH Papers.

39. Chambers, *Seedtime of Reform,* p. 137. See Herrick, "A Holy Discontent: The History of the New York City Social Settlements, 1919–1941," pp. 364–412.

40. Quoted in Helen Hall, "The Consequences of Social Action for the Group Work Agency," NCSW *Proceedings* (1936), p. 236.

41. The text of Helen Hall's address, as published in an abridged form in the NCSW *Proceedings* (1936), contains no direct mention of the suspicions of board members, the affluent and the poor regarding communist infiltration. The original unabridged text, found in the NFS Papers, refers explicitly to these fears. NFS Papers, Folder 82. The editors or perhaps the contributors of the *Proceedings* frequently published addresses that, through abridgement and emendation, were more diplomatic than the original texts.

42. NCL Papers, Boxes 93 and 94.

43. NLWV Papers, BM, L34.

44. Report of NYA Survey (Oct. 1940), p. 4, NYA Papers, Box 608.

CHAPTER 7

1. Samuel Mencher, "The Future of Voluntarism in American Social Welfare," in Alfred J. Kahn (ed.), *Issues in American Social Welfare* (New York: Columbia University Press, 1959), p. 291.

Index

Weston, S. Burns, 99–100, 111
Williams, Aubrey, 99
Works Progress Administration (Works Projects Administration, 1939), 23, 26, 29, 76, 83–84
World War I, 5
World War II, 102–103

YMCA, 3–5, 13–14, 25, 73–80, 84–86, 88–89, 91, 93, 96, 104–105, 107–108, 116
YWCA, 6, 9, 14, 25, 73–78, 84, 91, 93, 105–106, 113, 116
Youth work, 4, 75–79, 81, 84–93, 99–102, 106–107, 109